I would like to dedicate this book to my two babies, Victoria and Brooklyn, the two people who keep me strong and the two people I will love forever

David (Daddy)

Hodder & Stoughton

BECKHAM

DAVID BECKHAM MY WORLD PHOTOGRAPHY BY DEAN FREEMAN

First published in Great Britain in 2000
by Hodder and Stoughton
A division of Hodder Headline
First published in paperback in Great Britain in 2001
by Hodder and Stoughton
A division of Hodder Headline

A CIP catalogue record for this title is available from the
British Library

ISBN 0 340 79270 1

Printed and bound in Great Britain
by Butler & Tanner Ltd, Frome, Somerset

Hodder and Stoughton
A division of Hodder Headline
338 Euston Road
London NW1 3BH

CONTENTS

CHAPTER 1
FOOTBALL DAZE

All I ever wanted to do was kick a football about. It didn't enter my head to do anything else. I think I was programmed by my dad to some extent. I knew he wanted me to be a footballer and he encouraged me to play when I was a kid. I enjoyed playing, whether it was in the garden or on a pitch with the Sunday league team. It wasn't imposed on me, though, and I'm grateful for that. I had a friend who used to come to the park with us and his dad was really pushy. He was always saying, 'You can't do that, you've got to do this.' My mate could have been a good player, but he just stopped wanting to play and has never been involved in football since. I'm glad it didn't turn out that way for me, but I realise that things could easily have been so different.

The problem is that when you want something so badly, it can start to get on top of you. I'd always wanted to play for Man United and I don't know what would have happened if I hadn't been given the chance. Maybe I wouldn't have ended up in football at all. I've always loved the game, but being given the chance to play at Man United made the difference. When I had to make the decision about going to Manchester or staying in London and playing for Tottenham or Arsenal, my dad sat me down and said, 'These are the options. Here's what these people are offering you and this is what the others are offering.' We'd been up to Manchester, we'd been to Arsenal and Tottenham and he said, 'If you want to stay in London, then great. If you want to go up to Manchester, we'll be up every weekend watching you and supporting you. Just do what you want.'

For me, there was never any question of going to any other club. Still, if my parents hadn't been so supportive, I might not have been so ready to leave home at 16. I might even have rebelled, though I wasn't really that sort of person.

Somehow my parents found the right balance and my dad gave me a strong sense of ambition, without overdoing it. Having my parents' support has been invaluable. They've always been there for me. My dad has only missed one or two games in the last eight years, including away games. He's a self-employed gas engineer, so he can arrange his work around the matches. It's been a financial drain but he works hard and he's never missed a Saturday game.

My mum and dad always bought me a football for Christmas, as far back as I can remember. I also had a new Man United kit every year and my grandad, my mum's dad, always bought me the new Tottenham kit. I had to put the Tottenham kit on when I went up my nan and grandad's because it was my Christmas present and it made my grandad happy, but it didn't please my dad. There was always conflict there. My father's dad supported Arsenal and my dad hates Arsenal, so there was some rivalry between those two as well. I don't think I was pushed but my dad swayed me towards Man United. It was probably his greatest fear that I'd end up supporting Arsenal.

Dad played a lot of football himself. He always took me with him when he was playing and stayed behind to coach me for an hour afterwards. When I was 10 or 11, I was desperate to join in with him and his mates, but for ages he didn't let me because they were all too big. Eventually I was allowed to join in when he realised I could play a little bit.

The training he gave me as a kid has got me to where I am today. Since then I have always practised a lot. It is the only way to get to the top. Zinedine Zidane and Luis Figo are two of the best players in the world, but although they obviously have amazing natural talent, they would never have achieved what they have without years and years of practice.

When I score from way out, people often say that it is a freak goal but it isn't. I have worked on taking shots at goal from way out since I was a kid. I scored a couple of goals like that when I was playing for Ridgeway Rovers in the Sunday league. Even as a 13 year old, I could kick the ball a long way, further than most of the other kids, and I did it twice from the halfway line. I remember getting mobbed by my mates the first time. We have always tried spectacular shots like that in training at United and I scored goals like that a couple of times in reserve matches.

It is only by practising that you get to score the spectacular goals which give you such a buzz. The long-range shot at Wimbledon is my all-time favourite. I remember seeing Neil Sullivan off his line and thinking I might as well go for it. I didn't even think to look where I was on the pitch. It was only when I saw the video that I realised how far out I was. That video tape has got a bit of a hammering. I've still got the boots somewhere. I never wore them again after that goal.

I know my skills come from years of working with my dad in the local park. It all stems from how you are brought up. Sometimes you see Sunday league football with the players clattering into each other, but my dad taught me technique. If I am teaching kids, the most important thing I try to get across is to enjoy the game and enjoy learning skills. That was the great thing about playing with my dad. We would work on passing, crossing and shooting for hours and hours. He was the biggest influence on me and taught me everything I know.

I would be in our local park, Chase Lane, from as soon as I got home from school until 11 o'clock at night all through my school days. If I was on my own, I would play keepy-uppy for hours. My mum was happy because she could always be certain where I was. I knew that I would have to put that work in to make it into the Manchester United first team. It is exactly the same philosophy I have now.

My older sister Lynne always hated football, but my younger sister Joanne likes it. Lynne's now married with a two-year-old baby and Joanne works at Vidal Sassoon and lives at home. Joanne never used to miss a match and even when she started to get fed up with the football, she'd come because she liked all my friends. I've always felt very protective about her and I think Lynne's been protective of me in her own way. We went to the same school and if someone was having a go at me, she'd always stick up for me. Now that Lynne's settled down and I have my own life, we don't get the chance to see each other very often. I used to see Joanne every Saturday when I had a game but now she's at Vidal Sassoon, where Saturday's a big day, she often can't make it. I miss them both because we were very, very close. Joanne's got her own friends and has her own life to lead. Unfortunately for me, she often bumps into footballers from the London clubs when she goes out and it's a nightmare when she comes back and tells me her stories. Still, I just have to let her get on with it because otherwise I'd end up locking her inside the house. The best I can do is warn her!

As a kid one of my big treats was when my dad got tickets for a match. It was a lot easier to get them back then and he'd take me to any game he could, mostly at White Hart Lane. When I got more involved with football, West Ham were trying to get me to play for them, and so were Tottenham and Arsenal, so I started getting free tickets and we were able to go all the time.

Our biggest treat as a family was going to Southend. My mum and dad used to say, 'Right, we'll go this Saturday,' and we'd all get in the car and drive up there for the day. It was a few years ago when there wasn't so much fuss about how polluted the sea was, and we'd all go swimming. It was great fun, but it wasn't my favourite outing because I'd rather go over to the park and play football or watch a game.

Every Saturday morning I'd go to my nan and grandad's with my mum and sisters. Sometimes we used to go shopping but mostly I'd go to the park to play football. The park was right next to the block of flats where my nan and grandad lived, which meant my mum could keep an eye on me. I'd play football non-stop and then I'd come in and watch *Grandstand*.

Football was drummed into me and it was all I wanted to do, all I wanted to know. I suppose it was an easy way to win my parents' approval. That approval has always been important to me. I even worried about what my mum and dad would think about me getting my hair cut. They hated it at first because everyone had always known me as the lad with the blond floppy hair and they didn't want me to lose that image. But they've got used to it now and my mum is pleased that I don't have to tuck my hair behind my ears any more when I'm playing. She hated that habit.

I was a cub and later went on to be a scout, both of which involved football, so I was happy doing that. Also, we'd go camping and it was great to go away with a group of friends. You learn quite a bit about yourself when you're away from your family. I'd like to go camping with Victoria but it's probably not safe now. Still, maybe we'll get to go one day.

I absolutely adored training on a Wednesday night with my Sunday league football team. Once, my mum and dad stopped me going to training as a punishment for something. That killed me. It was the worst punishment I could ever have had. They quite often grounded me when I wanted to go out, usually because I'd come in late, at 10 or 10.30 when they'd told me to be home by 9. Most of the time I did what they wanted but I stepped out of line sometimes, like most kids.

I don't drink much but I can remember the first time I got drunk. It was on Christmas Eve when I was 15 and I went to a party with a couple of friends. I wasn't allowed to go to many places at that age, but my mum let me out this time. I was sick before I got home, so the worst was over but when I got in, I said I'd eaten something bad. They never realised I was drunk. It put me off drinking.

I had one really, really good friend called John at primary school, but when we moved on, we went to different schools and sort of split up. We were never as good friends again. I had other friends at school and out of school, but no one like him. I was just into my football too much. On a Saturday night, my friends would be on the corner of the street with a bottle of Woodpecker and a fag or going to house parties, but I'd be in watching *Match of the Day* and going to bed early because I had a game the next morning. Sometimes I did want to go out with them but most of the time I was happy staying in. It was the Sunday morning match I looked forward to, which meant taking it easy the night before.

The only job I've ever had, apart from football, was collecting glasses at the Walthamstow dog track when I was 11 or 12. I did it because I wanted extra pocket money. It was good money for my age, I was earning quite a bit and I did it with a couple of mates, so it was fun.

I used to do every sport going at school. I'd get involved in anything, from rounders, baseball and softball to athletics and basketball. I played rugby every now and again and we used to do some swimming too, so I was a bit of an all-rounder. I didn't like being in the classroom much. I think it's important to get a good education, but football was the only thing on my mind. It was all I ever wanted to do. I wasn't very interested in school, so I can't remember much about the lessons, except for the art classes which I enjoyed. I don't want it to be like that for Brooklyn. We're already trying to read him books even though he's far too young to sit still for long enough. I hope the fact that he usually wants to eat them or kick them around on the floor doesn't mean that he takes after me in that way.

CHAPTER 2
THERE'S ONLY ONE MAN UNITED

Leaving school was a bit of a relief and anyway I was going to Manchester to live my dream of playing for Man United. It wasn't too hard leaving home because I still saw a lot of my parents. I loved living in digs, even though I was kicked out of the first two places I stayed. I had to leave the first one because the lad I was staying with did something wrong and the landlady decided to chuck us both out. She was very strange. She used to lock the kitchen up at night so that we couldn't go down and get something to eat, but one night my mate sneaked down to get some food and got caught. That was that. In the second digs, I said the food wasn't very good, so the landlady decided to kick me out. The third place was perfect. The landlord and landlady, Annie and Tommy Kay, were absolutely brilliant. It was like having another mum and dad. I was with them for two and a half years and they made me feel at home and settled, so I could really concentrate on my football.

By the time I left them I was 19. I was earning a bit more money and it was time to start branching out. One of my friends lived in an area where there were some new properties going up and I went down to see one of them. It was a bit more than I wanted to pay but I absolutely loved it so I bought it. It was a great bachelor pad. It had three storeys and the top floor was just one bedroom, with a massive window. It was the first house Victoria came up to when I met her. I had a few parties there before I met Victoria and she and I had a party there after a Spice Girls concert a couple of years ago, with all the other Girls, a lot of my friends and our mums and dads. I had some fun times there.

When I first arrived at Man United it was a bit scary, partly because all my heroes were from United. I had their pictures on my bedroom wall — Steve Bruce, Gordon Strachan and especially Bryan Robson. I had a shirt with his name on. I was picked to go for a trial at 13, and after that I went up to Manchester every summer. I couldn't wait to be part of it. Most of the young lads would come in and out over the holidays, but I was determined to stay for all six weeks because I loved it so much. I stayed in the halls of residence in Salford with about 30 lads. I don't know what happened to the rest of them but as far as I know, none of them ended up in the Premier League.

The great thing about it was that all the players involved were made to feel part of a family. Everyone knew the young kids' names, which was a great feeling. I remember the first time I went up there Alex Ferguson knew my name and that has a real effect on you. Bryan Robson was the one I always wanted to meet, just to listen to, even if I couldn't talk to him. Ryan Giggs and Lee Sharpe were also coming through at the time and we all felt part of the group.

We used to look up to the senior players even when we were breaking into the first team. You have to have that respect. It's hard to believe that there are now young kids looking up to me like that. It's also a real honour, but very strange, when an older person who's been around for much longer than I have, is looking up to me.

Eric Cantona and Peter Schmeichel were the big legends when I was coming through and they each had an amazing aura. You would notice them just walking into the room. I probably chatted more with Peter. Eric's English wasn't great and he would keep himself to himself quite a lot whereas Peter is really outgoing, as everyone knows. You could talk to him about life and your family because he was so approachable. After I got my head shaved I spoke to him on the phone and he slaughtered me about it.

Eric was much harder to get to know. It was a shame when he left but I could understand the way he went without warning. He is totally his own man and was always the type to do surprising things. I know that Eric had to put up with a lot of abuse just because he was the best, which is terrible. He came back to watch the Tottenham Hotspur game at the end of the 1999-2000 season when we received the championship trophy. It was great to see him but we didn't talk for long. He never said too much. He led by example.

Now there are so many players from other countries playing in the Premiership that I think things have got a lot better when it comes to prejudice within football. Black and Asian players used to get a lot more abuse, especially at certain grounds. The campaign against racism within football over the last five or six years has made a difference, not just in club sides, but in international sides as well. I've been lucky in that none of the managers I've played under have given the impression that they feel any differently about black, white or Asian players. It would make me feel very uncomfortable if they did because I'm not racist in any way. I think everyone should be allowed to do what they want to do without people making an issue out of colour. I feel very strongly about that.

People think that footballers are macho homophobic beer drinkers, but it doesn't bother me one bit whether someone's gay or straight. Being around the world of showbusiness has probably made me look at sexuality in a different way, and I was brought up not to be prejudiced about other people. I think your attitude to things like that often stems from your family.

Cantona was a big influence at Old Trafford, especially the way he used to stay behind after training to work on skills. I have done that all my life. I used to find a bag of balls and take free kicks and corners until the training staff ordered me in. I have always felt I could get better and that has never changed. It's not a case of waking up one morning and thinking I need to work on this or that — I have worked on all my weaknesses ever since I was a kid to try to achieve a general improvement in all my skills.

Eric joined the club just two months after I made my first-team debut. It was at Brighton in the League Cup in September 1992 and I was thrown in as a 17 year old. I had been training with the first team and playing well in the reserves but never gave myself a chance of a game. I remember it well because we travelled down there in a tiny plane and it was a terrible flight. We stayed in the Grand Hotel, the one that got bombed by the IRA when the Conservative Party was staying there. It was a night match and I remember sitting there terrified that I might get on. Next thing I know, I have taken Andrei Kanchelskis's place. Paul Ince, Danny Wallace and players like that were in the team. I've still got the shirt. We didn't get many at the time and that one meant a lot to me and especially to my parents. They travelled pretty much to every United match, even when they were not expecting me to get a game. They were really surprised when I came on.

After that, I was back on the fringes for a couple of years. Alex Ferguson has said that I was a later developer than some of the others and that is why he sent me out on loan to Preston when I was 19. I was shocked when I first heard that I was going out on loan. I thought it was a sign that a club was trying to get rid of a player. It was only when I talked to the manager and he explained why he wanted me to go to Preston that I understood. He said that it might be good for me to go and get some first team experience and, after that chat, I was really up for it, even though it did mean going from the Premiership to the third division.

It was one of the best things I have ever done. It's not like Preston are a small club but, at United, you get used to having the best of everything, perfect training pitches, your kit washed and ironed. You go to somewhere like Preston and you realise life is not all like that. When I turned up on the first day I didn't have any kit with me and I bet the other players thought I was a right flash sod. I was driving a Ford Escort at the time but I was from Manchester United so they thought I must be a bit big-time. I was offered the option of training with United and just turning up for Preston matches, or training with them all week. The fact that I turned up at Preston every day made them realise that I didn't think I was too good to talk to them. I went to local presentations with the rest of the players and, after the first game, I think they realised I was there to work. The manager, Gary Peters, was great with me and so were the players, including David Moyes who is the manager there now.

It probably helped that I scored on my debut, straight from a corner. It was March 1995 and I came on at home to Doncaster Rovers and curled one straight in with my right foot to get us a 2-2 draw. I started the next match against Fulham and scored in that as well, with a free kick from outside the box. They had Terry Hurlock playing for them and I remember being a bit worried about myself. He was known as a hard-man and, even though I'm slim now, I was a right skinny kid then. But he left me alone and I remember really enjoying myself. I was almost disappointed to get called back to Old Trafford after five games, although I wasn't upset for long.

The manager was short of midfield players so, after playing for Preston at Lincoln City on one Saturday, the next week I was playing in front of more than 40,000 at home to Leeds United with Paul Ince and Mark Hughes. It was the season United missed out on the title to Blackburn Rovers, which was a massive disappointment for everyone but at least I had started to break into the first team.

When the 1995-96 season started, I had played more league matches for Preston than United so I never imagined that I would play more than 30 games and be part of a double-winning team in my first full year. The manager had made big sacrifices by selling Mark Hughes, Paul Ince and Andrei Kanchelskis over the summer. I think everyone was surprised. Incey was at the top of his career, playing well and winning things with United. But that just showed the faith that the boss had in the young lads and it made you want to repay it.

The manager never made a big deal about it. He never called us together and said 'this is your big chance to prove yourselves' but we all knew we had to. Although I scored in the opening game at Aston Villa, we lost and Alan Hansen famously said that you can't win anything with kids. That really made us aware of how much we had to do, but we had faith in ourselves as a team despite what Hansen said. That comes from playing together for years. You always have a few doubts but you have to lose them quickly playing at a club like United because otherwise you would crack under the pressure.

It probably helped me that lads I had grown up with such as Nicky Butt and Gary Neville were already in the team. I lacked size and physical presence then, which was probably why they were selected for the first team ahead of me. I am not the biggest now but at least I can take care of myself and give it back. In those days I would get muscled out a few times. I got done by most of them at some stage but I clearly remember Stuart Pearce playing for Nottingham Forest. It was one of my first games and I was pretty nervous coming up against him with his sleeves rolled up and his reputation. Not long into the game he whacked me right up into the air and left me in a heap on the grass. He didn't say anything. He didn't have to. It was just his way of letting me know he was around.

I used to do a certain amount of work on the weights and I filled out anyway, but a lot of it comes from confidence. Playing in a successful team always gives you confidence. All the young lads looked after each other and, whether you were right or wrong, they would stick up for you. That is something that goes right through the club, not just from the manager but also the rest of the staff. Everyone talks about the 'hairdryer' treatment from the manager but you would also get that in the youth team from Eric Harrison, the youth-team coach. He makes sure that you know what the standards are going to be on and off the pitch, if you do ever make it up to the first team.

I have never been a big drinker. I wasn't an angel but the only real tellings off I got were for stuff on the field. I remember a youth-team game against Liverpool. It was a big match and Eric Harrison gave me a right going over, saying that I was playing 'Hollywood passes'. I was showboating, hitting flash, stupid balls and he brought me down a few pegs.

No one is ever allowed to get too big-time at United. At Old Trafford, you have to remember that all the big players leave and the club goes on. Cantona, Ince, Schmeichel, Hughes and Robson have been through the door and the team goes from success to success. They are still respected and loved by everyone at Old Trafford but the club has to move on. We have all grown up knowing that, and it will be the same when I move on. That doesn't worry me, it just keeps me on my toes. It is all part of why we have won so much over the years.

The atmosphere at the club is very focused and positive. We train very hard and that is another reason why we have been so successful. Good training is so important and I have been lucky to work with some of the best — Eric Harrison, Brian Kidd and Steve McClaren. They have all got slightly different methods but the most important thing is that they never let you get bored. They are always thinking of new ways to teach you skills. If you are working every day, you have to keep players occupied.

Steve McClaren introduced a few new things. On a Friday, he used to line all the players up on the halfway line and when he shouted an instruction like 'go left', you had to do the opposite. It doesn't sound too complicated but it catches you out if you haven't slept well. The players who get it wrong end up in the final and you don't want to lose that. If you do, the prize is a T-shirt with 'I've had a Pally' or 'I've had a Neville' on it — Gary Pallister always used to be the worst and Phil isn't much better. If you lose three times, you get to keep the shirt forever. It is those little things which help keep us in good spirits.

I like to vary my training from day to day. Sometimes if I am a bit bored I will practise my free kicks with bare feet. I used to kick around barefoot when I was younger. It can help your feel for the ball. I don't think the England physio was too keen when he saw me doing it in training during Euro 2000. It is just something I have always liked to do. My grandad used to go mad at me because

I was always kicking things around in the garden at home and he used to look after it. He didn't like it when his flowers got ruined.

I know some people say my left foot isn't as good as it could be or my heading could be stronger. It is not for lack of practice and I don't believe I am bad at either. I can use my left foot but it makes more sense to use my right when I can because that is the stronger one.

The whip I get on free kicks is something I have always practised. I think that it is an ability you are born with, but I still work hard to improve it. I am sure that Denis Irwin and Alessandro Del Piero, who can both do it really well, do the same.

Roberto Carlos has an amazing ability with free kicks and he and Bixente Lizerazu, the France left-back who plays for Bayern Munich, are the two toughest defenders I have ever faced. If I had to name just one, it would be Roberto Carlos. That may seem a strange choice because he is not as good a defender as Lizerazu but he is so quick that it doesn't matter. He puts you on the back foot by being quicker than just about anybody on the pitch. That is his strength. The European Cup quarter-final against Real Madrid at the Bernabeu in April 2000 was one of the toughest matches I have played because Roberto Carlos has such quick feet and he breaks forward whenever he can. If you are not careful, you spend all night chasing back after him.

Another hard game was against Borussia Dortmund in the European Cup semi-final in April 1997 when Jorg Heinrich was left wing-back for the German club. It was the first time I had come up against him and I found it really tough, but he was not as dangerous when I faced him playing against Fiorentina in the 1999-2000 competition. He sat off me and gave me a lot of room.

I have improved a lot in the five years since I started playing regularly for the first team and I am still maturing into a better player. You learn to take more control of a game, although pacing myself has never been a problem. I was county 1500m champion for four years on the trot and won a lot of cross-country races when I was at school so I have always had good stamina. Steve McClaren brought in some equipment once that measured how far each player had run during a game and I came out highest with over 14km. Since I was a kid I have always been able to run all day and United fans appreciate it when they see players working hard. They have always demanded that the team goes flat out.

That comes from your desire as well and, despite what people say about my temper, I don't think I have done anything worse than be competitive. I want to win at everything and that is something that I was brought up to believe. I don't think I could have achieved what I have in my career without it. My dad has had a word a few times about calming down and not making myself look silly. I understand why, although he's got a bit of a cheek because he used to react. That's probably where I got it from. When he was playing Sunday league, he would always give it back, and I think he had a bit of trouble with discipline, that and offside. They used to call him the Offside King and they even made a trophy for him.

Gary Neville is my best mate at the club and he will tell me if he thinks I have done something wrong. He is a great friend to have because he is totally straight and gives you good advice. But it is not as if I am some playboy footballer or a bad influence. I have been sent off twice in my professional career and have never been involved in fighting or anything like that on or off the pitch.

Desire and determination are what make United the club it is. A mate of mine plays in the Sunday league and he says his manager is always trying to get his players to copy our spirit. There have been times when we have gone over the top. The manager had a go at us when we complained to the referee about a penalty given to Middlesbrough at Old Trafford. We got a bit carried away and he told us so, but it was a sign of how badly we want to win and how we all stick together.

I do have flashes of temper but that is part of what makes me the player I am. People talk about me sometimes as though I am getting sent off all the time but it has only happened once in a United shirt, in Brazil. We were playing against a Mexican side, Necaxa, in the Maracana, which is as special as playing at any of the great grounds in Europe.

I could see why the referee sent me off when I watched it on television but at the time I thought it was harsh. I had my foot up but I wasn't trying maliciously to hurt the player. It is not in my nature to go around hurting people. I was trying to get the ball and when he put his leg up as well it looked like a stamp. It wasn't a great tackle but it was a genuine one, but yet again it became a big issue about my temperament. If you look at my disciplinary record, I don't think there is a problem at all. The manager wants players with a bit of fire in them, not players who are going to give up and walk away.

Without any doubt much of the success of United is down to Alex Ferguson. My relationship with him has always been one of great respect. We've had a couple of well-publicised bust-ups but I have so much to thank him for, which is something people often choose to forget.

The great thing about him is that you can have a blazing face-to-face row but it will be forgotten 24 hours later, provided that you pull your weight. I don't think there has been a player through Old Trafford who has not had a rollocking from him, but you can hardly complain when you see what he's won in his career. Sometimes it is better that people let off steam, especially at a football club where there is so much pressure on everybody.

The manager has never been one to socialise with the players. I have never been round to his house or anything like that and I don't see that changing. But that doesn't mean I didn't invite him to my wedding. I was disappointed that he couldn't come because of a family wedding of his own. I've willingly gone to him in the past with my personal problems, and when Victoria and I heard the news that she was pregnant, he was one of the first people I told outside the family. He was as chuffed for us as anyone. I think he likes the players to settle down.

I know he thought I spent too much time on the phone to Victoria when we first started seeing each other. I remember he pulled me aside once and had a quiet word about it. It was in 1998 when Victoria had gone to the States to work and I was missing her. I am always on the phone, whether it is to Victoria or my mates or family. That time she went away, my mobile bill was over £2,000 for the month. It was an obscene amount and I cut down after that.

The bust-ups with the manager were blown out of all proportion and people started making ridiculous assumptions that we never get on. There was one after I went to a party in London last season which was my fault and I apologised. We were flying out to Austria from Manchester on a Tuesday morning for a Champions League match against Sturm Graz on the

Wednesday and I went to a party in London hosted by Jade Jagger on the Monday night. Jade had given us a beautiful picture as a wedding present and Victoria and I wanted to support her at a launch party for her work in the St Martin's Lane Hotel. I should have known that going out two days before a big game was wrong, even if I was not drinking. It came out in the papers that I left at midnight. In fact, I was out of there by 9.30 and the strongest thing I drank was cranberry juice.

Before the game in Austria, the manager pulled me and said he wanted a word afterwards. I went to see him and said, 'Sorry, I shouldn't have gone and it won't happen again.' That was the end of it as far as we were both concerned although I also got fined one week's wages. For all the reputation as a troublemaker that some people try to portray, that was only the second time I have ever been fined at United. I should know because I check my financial details closely every week and they take it straight off your salary. That should have been the end of it but the publicity made it ten times worse. It was mostly because I was wearing a bandana, which became front-page news, but it had been forgotten by the manager and me long before the papers were finished with it.

The other famous occasion was the Leeds United match in February when I was left in the stands after I missed training on the Friday morning. Brooklyn had been ill and I think any parent will tell you that you are paranoid with your first baby. You worry about any little thing that might be wrong with him so when he went pale and then started being sick in the early hours, there was no way I was going to leave him. I was worried for him and when morning came I felt I needed to be looking after him and I rang the club to tell them. I spoke to Steve McClaren and explained what had happened. I honestly thought that nothing more would be said.

I certainly didn't expect the reaction I got when I turned up at training on the Saturday morning. I didn't think it would be a big deal but I found out straightaway that the manager wasn't happy. I went out to train and we had a big row on the pitch. I think the other players were shocked because it just went off completely and things were said pretty bluntly. I am not going into details because, at United, we keep these things private, but there was a bit of swearing and then he told me to leave.

It was written at the time that I had stormed away from the club. I did get in my car to drive away because the manager had told me to get out, but I barely got much further than the gates outside the training ground in Carrington. I had had a few seconds to cool down and I thought it would be best if I went back and did some training on my own. Whatever had been said, I think I am professional about how I go about my job and I wanted to give myself every chance of playing against Leeds. I turned my car around and went back into the gym and did some work on the exercise bike.

I still thought I might have a chance of playing against Leeds United because the manager hadn't said that I wouldn't, but I found out first thing when we reported on the Sunday morning that I wasn't playing. I turned up to travel with the team as usual but on the coach on the way over to Elland Road, I discovered that I wasn't even going to be on the bench. Obviously it wasn't easy to take. I felt I hadn't done anything wrong and I hate not playing at the best of times, but there was nothing I could do about it apart from sit in the stands and hope the team won.

Anyone who thinks that I didn't want United to win that day doesn't have a clue about me or the relationship in the United dressing room. There were loads of pictures in the papers the next day of me not looking happy but that is hardly surprising when you are not playing in one of the biggest games of the season. It is not easy having all those camera lenses sticking up at you in the stands when there is a big game happening on the pitch, but when the game kicked off, my priority was hoping that we would beat Leeds. It was a massive game because they were our main rivals in the championship race. We knew if we could beat them that it would kill them off, mentally as much as anything, because it would show them that we were not going to buckle. Andy Cole scored to give us a 1-0 victory and I was as happy as anyone that we had come through it.

There was typical over-reaction, saying that I was finished at United and that I would have to move abroad. I didn't believe most of it, but it is still not easy to take when everyone is talking about it and you know that you cannot pick up a paper without seeing it. Luckily the manager doesn't bear grudges so I was pretty sure it would all be sorted out. He is strict about things but I was just thinking about my little boy. Football is important but family always comes first. Victoria and I both stayed with Brooklyn because he was ill and we were very worried. Children do bounce back very quickly from minor illnesses and by the afternoon on the Friday, he was better.

It had been well documented by then that I had bought a house near London and some people used the story as an excuse to say that I was spending too much time down there and would be signing for Arsenal. Some of the stories even suggested that Victoria was pressurising me to make a move. That is ridiculous. She is very supportive of what I do and would never be as selfish as to suggest I move clubs for her convenience. The truth is that I have never spent more than a handful of days a month down south because I know travelling affects my football. There were even stories that I had bought a Jeep that had a custom-built bed in it so I could be driven up and down to training and sleep on the way. Then there was the one about buying a helicopter that could land at the training ground.

The ridiculous thing is that I would have had to be mad to stay in Hertfordshire for many nights. It will take months to do up the house and it was like a bomb site for ages after we bought it. There is no way I could spend that much time there even if I wanted to and I would never take the chance of messing with my football. We do enough travelling as it is, so I know how a three-hour coach journey can take it out of you. The hard thing for me has been getting that message over to the United supporters because I never want them thinking that I am not committed to the club.

My relationship with Alex Ferguson now is as good as ever. The whole incident when I missed training would never even have come out like it did if there had not been a photographer hiding in the bushes outside the training ground. I know the manager would have done his best to keep it all in-house. I doubt he would have given his version of events in his book if the story had not been done to death in the papers. We had a disagreement but you forget it and get on with your job.

There have been all sorts of rumours about the manager and Victoria not getting on but it is news to us. I can understand if he was nervous at first about one of his players going out with a pop star but you can't help who you fall in love with, and I think whatever reservations he might have had, he is basically happy to see his players settle down.

The trouble is that it is impossible to stop the gossip. There was the evening of his testimonial dinner in Manchester when Victoria and I turned up a little bit late and it came out that we were snubbing him and stealing the attention. The truth is that we were late because the babysitter we employed that night couldn't get Brooklyn to sleep. We always like to make sure he's asleep before we leave him but he was very restless and we set off late. A little thing like that suddenly becomes a big story and it is totally untrue.

The manager has always supported me when it really matters and I read a bit in his autobiography where he said that, when it comes down to football, I will never let him down. As far as I am concerned, that is all that matters. If I give him and the club everything as a player then we will always have that mutual respect. It is not as if I have been a nightmare to control. One sending off in my United career in the eight years since I made my debut hardly makes me a troublemaker and I have always given my all.

I trust the manager to make the right decisions for me now as much as I did when I signed for the club as a teenager and put my career in his hands. I have worked hard to get where I am today but I am not sure if I would have done it without the manager's help. Without him, I might easily not be the same player because you cannot help but learn from his competitive spirit. People might say that you should take that for granted in a professional sportsman but that isn't always the case and it is the manager who has created United's will to win by getting together the right type of players. He doesn't have favourites, which builds a good atmosphere. It hasn't done any of us badly so far.

The bottom line is that, for all the ups and downs, you know that he is making his football decisions for the right reasons. He is a hard man and there have been all sorts of disagreements but a player only has to worry about himself and he has a whole team to think about. I think I respond to that type of management because my dad has a similar personality to Alex Ferguson. He can be tough on me but that has always stood me in good stead to deal with whatever problems have come up in my career. I will always be grateful to them both.

CHAPTER 3
MY FIRST TEAM

Nothing compares to what I've got with Victoria and that's why I married her. I see us as the perfect couple. The way we are always holding hands and kissing and being affectionate towards each other is just the way we both are naturally. We don't do it for show. We're like that when we are indoors watching a video, or even when we're just having a cup of tea. We always want to sit or stand next to each other, wherever we are.

If I wasn't a footballer and Victoria wasn't a pop star, I would probably have gone back to my mates after I'd met her and told them about the size of my new girlfriend's house or her swimming pool. Still, I'd be lying if I didn't admit that being a pop star was a part of the attraction. That did it for me and likewise, the fact that I was good at my job was part of the attraction for her. We were both successful and could relate to each other as equals. I would have been attracted to her physically even if we hadn't been in the situation that we were in. Strangely though, she wasn't what I thought of as my type. I always used to go out with blonde girls. In fact, she was the first dark-haired girl I'd ever been out with, so it's weird that I ended up marrying her.

When the Spice Girls first appeared, all the lads had their favourite. One of my mates used to say, 'Geri's the one. Geri's definitely the one. Look at her, yeah,' and I'd say, 'No, believe me, the one with the dark hair, the bob, is the one. The one with the legs.' Then Victoria turned up at a football game in London. I sort of said hi, but she was more forward than I was and came up to me and said hello. Then the Spice Girls' manager at the time introduced us properly. I'm a shy person, so I still only managed to say hello and then turned away. I was cursing myself afterwards because I just couldn't believe that I'd wasted my big chance.

A few weeks later, she turned up in Manchester. After the match, I went to get a drink in the players' lounge and saw her out of the corner of my eye, walking over to the bar. I'd got my drink, so I was already walking away from the bar by then. Later she said that I'd practically ignored her as I went by, just mumbling something like, 'Hi, are you all right?' as I passed her. That was that, again.

She was convinced at this point that I didn't want to know her, but the truth was that I was very shy. Luckily, she'd had a couple of glasses of wine, so she had the courage to come over and we started talking. I felt self-conscious because I could see everyone watching us, but soon we were chatting away. Once I get going, I'm all right. It's only at the beginning of a conversation that I find it hard to talk to someone I don't know. By the end, we were the only ones left in the lounge. Finally, Victoria turned round and said something like, 'So, are you going to give me your number?'

She later told me that she felt really let down when I said I wanted to take her number instead because she thought it was a brush-off. I just wanted her number because I was worried that she would take mine and not ring me. I told her I would call the next morning at 11. When I got home I wrote her number down on six or seven bits of paper around the house so that I wouldn't lose it.

I actually rang her earlier than 11 because I was training that morning. She was going away the next day and I wanted to drive to London to see her before she went. She wanted me to come down, too, but she wouldn't ask me and I wouldn't ask her. I was skirting around it by asking her what she was doing and stuff like that.

Apparently she got off the phone and said, 'I'm dying for him to come down!' A bit later I plucked up the courage and rang her back. I said as casually as I could that I wasn't doing anything that evening and if she maybe wanted to go out, then we could. I drove down to London that day and we went out in the evening — only we didn't go anywhere because we couldn't be seen out together.

Obviously, going out with a Spice Girl was a big deal. I was a footballer but I was nothing compared to Victoria at that point, so it was quite a big thing just being with her. That first evening, she said, 'Let's pop round one of my friend's houses. It's quiet there and we can sit down and have a drink in peace.' When I walked in, the friend was Melanie C. So I'm thinking, oh my God! It made it worse that she had Liverpool posters on the wall. I thought, what am I going to do? Victoria went into the kitchen to say something to Melanie. I don't know what she was saying, but I was sitting there in the living room thinking, get me out of here, please. I was so nervous.

Melanie was brilliant, though. All the Girls have been fantastic. It must have been hard at first because they're unbelievably protective of each other, just as I'm protective of my friends. When I first met them, they were quite wary of me because I was trying to impress them and they were looking out for Victoria's best interests. It was very important to me that they liked me and got used to me and didn't think I was with Victoria just because she was a Spice Girl. I think they've got used to me now. I've always tried to keep out of the way of what goes on in the group and even in the beginning I didn't tell my friends anything. I didn't even tell my best mate Dave Gardiner that I'd spoken to Victoria and gone down to see her. He still teases me about that. When the news broke about us being together, everyone I knew wanted to know what the other Girls were like and what they said to me when I met them.

Now I get on really well with all of them. They've all been kind to me, great in fact, and they're all a good laugh. We don't get as much chance to meet up with them now because Victoria and I are so busy, but we occasionally go round to their houses for dinner. Victoria obviously sees much more of them than I do because I'm in Manchester most of the time.

Mel B is the total opposite of me. When I go to a club, I don't mind dancing if I feel like it and if I don't feel like it, I won't. But Melanie's the sort who drags you up by your hair and tries to make you dance if she likes a song, which I absolutely hate. And she's always doing it! Still, she's terrific and there aren't many people like her. She always speaks her mind and she's very impulsive but that's great.

Melanie C's been lovely to me since the day I met her. I didn't know how she'd be with me, being a Liverpool fan, because she does take her football seriously. But she's always been brilliant. She's very sincere and she's got her head screwed on the right way, like all the Girls. They always know what's going on around them, which is the way it should be.

Emma's quiet and shy, although not as shy as I am. She's probably the quietest of the three. She's always got a smile. I like being around all three of them. I'm still shy in front of them. I won't go in a room and start kissing them all and saying hello and starting conversations, but I'm relaxed enough to be in the same room as them and not sweat.

When the Girls get talking, I often leave the room. A lot of things get said, just like they do in the Man United changing room, and sometimes I just don't want to hear it or know what's going on.

Victoria was different from the girls I'd gone out with before. It was hard not to feel self-conscious with someone I'd seen on TV and I kept thinking, maybe I shouldn't say that or do this. But Victoria put me at ease straightaway. She was outgoing and funny and quite loud, which took the pressure off me.

It was difficult when Victoria and I first got together because the Girls are so high profile. We knew that once anyone found out it would be quite big news. We did manage to keep it quiet for the first month and a half, which was hard work but made it all quite exciting. Our first real date was at the pictures. I parked my car in central London and Victoria's driver drove us to the cinema to see Jerry McGuire. I wanted to hold Victoria's hand from the start and some girls don't like that, but that's the way I am. At the cinema, I tried to put my hand on her knee but I didn't want to be too forward on our first date, so I pretended I'd done it by accident. We were like two nervous teenagers.

It wasn't long before I fell in love with Victoria. I even felt a little bit in love when we went out on our first proper date. It was love but it was also a case of feeling, I really fancy this girl, there's something happening here. I felt that straightaway. I believe it was fate that we got together. There was a moment when Victoria said something that made me feel special. It was something that no one had ever said to me before. It wasn't anything out of the ordinary, just something nice, and it caught me. That was it. Game over.

Our first public date was in Manchester. There were rumours flying around about us but no one had any concrete evidence, so the papers couldn't say anything until then. A few weeks later, I went up to London and bought Victoria a handbag while I was out shopping. It wasn't her birthday or anything and she said she'd never been given anything like that before. About a week after that, I was back in London looking for an outfit to wear to meet her that evening. She was also out shopping with her sister and at one point she called up and said, 'Let's meet up quickly now, before you come and pick me up tonight.' So I pulled up by the side of the road next to her car and she jumped out with a massive bunny she'd bought me in Harrods. That was the sort of thing that got me. When I was walking back to the car, she said, 'Nice arse!' and that got me as well.

We both knew we had something special. It was all a question of whether we were able to make the time to see each other. A lot of people have to spend time apart from each other and don't make the effort but we made it work because we had such strong feelings for each other. I hated not seeing Victoria but I would have done anything to make it work. Absolutely anything.

Victoria was just more gorgeous than the rest, in every way. I proposed to her on 24 January 1998. We'd been seeing each other for six months. I'd asked her to go away for the weekend to a hotel just outside Cheshunt. We had a fantastic meal in the room, drank champagne and then I got down on one knee and proposed to her. We had talked generally about getting married, but she didn't know I was going to propose right then. She was a bit shocked and then she made me do it again!

One of the reasons we get on so well is that we believe in being faithful. We trust each other and that's a big thing in both our lives. It's absolutely necessary because we're away from each other quite a bit. That trust has always been there and it always will be. I think we're like that because we've been brought up that way. Our own parents are still together and you generally carry through the morals and example your family give you. We both realise that if you want to be with someone, you've got to be with just that person to make it work.

We're both a little bit jealous at times, though. It's inevitable because we're supposed to be a heart-throb and a sex symbol. Victoria is one of the most famous women in the world and she's gorgeous, so she's always going to have men looking at her. It's something I've come to terms with but it's still hard. I think it is difficult for anyone when a lot of people pay attention to the person they love, but I'm honoured that people think Victoria is so beautiful, so in that way it's great. If someone in the paper says they like her I always think, well you can like her, but sorry mate, you're too late.

There's always talk about how Victoria is in control and bosses me about, but we both wear the trousers in our relationship. We have an equal say in things. People think Victoria's in control because she's much more outspoken than I am and I'd rather sit in the background a lot of the time, but in fact there's a good balance in our relationship.

We both love children and so it was logical that we wanted to move on to the next level and have a child. It's the best thing we could have done. I look at Brooklyn and think his ears are like mine and his nose is like yours, he comes from the combination of our love.

I was probably the happiest person in the world when Victoria told me she was pregnant. It was unbelievable. I cried tears of joy. I went to every scan and Victoria bought me a couple of books and videos to watch, so I would be well prepared for it, although I must admit I didn't actually get through the videos. I don't mind if it's my own wife but I wasn't that keen on seeing other women giving birth. The books were better. We read a book that charted the development of the baby, day-by-day. We'd pick it up and say things like, 'Look, it's got its fingernails today!' The scans were amazing. I was away with England for the first one but when I told the manager about it, he let me off for a few hours. We didn't go to any antenatal classes, though. We always said we were going to, but we never got round to it.

The night before Brooklyn was born, I was playing in a big European game against Inter Milan at Old Trafford. An hour before the game, Victoria told me she had just had a twinge. I didn't know what to do, because if the baby was really on its way, I would be straight down to London to be with Victoria. Luckily, it was a false alarm and I was able to play the match. The next day, as I was on my way down to London, she told me that the doctor wanted us to go into hospital that afternoon. I remember it so clearly. I was eating a Lion Bar at the time, driving along the M6, and suddenly I felt like being sick with excitement, thinking oh my God, here we go!

It's a worrying time, although you're obviously hoping that things will go smoothly, which they did in the end. Victoria was worried about Brooklyn being all right, just like any mother with her first baby, and I was anxious but I felt deep down that everything was going to be okay. I was there during the Caesarean and saw everything and all the while Victoria kept saying how hungry she was. We both go through phases of liking certain foods and at that point she was into salmon. All she could talk about was how she couldn't wait to have some salmon, which was pretty funny considering what was going on.

Then I saw Brooklyn's head come out and heard him crying. Victoria couldn't hold him because the anaesthetic for the Caesarean meant that she couldn't feel anything from the neck down. So I was the first to hold him and it was unbelievable. It was weird, the best feeling in the world and like nothing I had ever felt before.

I thought then, as I do now, that as long as Brooklyn has a happy life and enjoys himself and stays healthy, like everyone else in my family, I'll be happy. That's all you can ask for as a parent. If he wants to go into football, then I'd love him to but whatever he wants to do, as long as he's happy, that's fine by me.

If anyone ever asked me whether they should have a child, I wouldn't hesitate in saying yes. You cannot imagine until you've been through it how special it is and how much you will love the baby. It's the best thing in the world. Having Brooklyn made me grow up and appreciate the little things in life. I used to worry about things that now seem so unimportant.

I've been totally involved with Brooklyn since day one and I do anything that needs to be done for him. I think that's the way it should be. When Victoria is working, I'll take him out with me for the day. I'm not bothered about feeding or changing nappies. I actually like doing those things. Brooklyn's amazing. Little things he does remind me of things I used to do and my parents say he reminds them of me when I was his age. It's great getting home in the afternoons after a stressful day to see him.

I'd always wanted a tattoo but I just couldn't decide what to have done until Brooklyn was born. My dad has a few tattoos on his arms, which is probably why I grew up wanting one. He had his first one when he was 13 and his dad nearly killed him for it. He's never pushed me to have one done. He's never even talked about it.

Having Brooklyn made my mind up that I wanted his name on me. A short while after I'd had that done, I was out with Victoria, Gary Neville and his girlfriend, Hannah, and I told them I really wanted another tattoo and asked them what they thought I should have done. So we hit on the idea of a male guardian angel on my back. Something that would look cool but would also mean something to me. It symbolises a free spirit. Once we have more children, I'll have tattoos of each of their names put just under the angel, so that they'll have him looking over them. The writing won't be the same size as the Brooklyn tattoo, though. I'm glad I had it that size, but I don't think I could have another three or four names that big on my back. I'll just have some explaining to do when they're older and they ask why Brooklyn's name is bigger than theirs.

I think a tattoo has to mean something more than just being a fashion statement. Both of my tattoos mean something to me, so I know for a fact that I'll never regret them. They represent the permanent things in my life. That's why I still want something to do with Victoria tattooed on me, although I haven't decided what and where yet.

Victoria doesn't want me to have any more but they're very addictive. People used to tell me that and now I've realised it's true. After I had the angel done, I got up from the bed and there were teeth marks in the pillow. I was sweating and shaking from two and a half hours of pain and I swore I would never have any more tattoos done because it absolutely killed me. But a week later, I got the urge to have another one. It's a weird feeling. Maybe I want more because I'm so fond of the ones I've actually got. Although it hurts to have them done, it's worth it because they are there forever and so are the feelings behind them. Still, Victoria says my back will look like a piece of scrap paper if I have any more.

I haven't encouraged Victoria to have a tattoo because I think it's something that she might regret. If she had one on the top of her shoulder and we were going out somewhere special and she had to wear a dress but the tattoo was only half showing under the straps, she might wish she'd never had it done. If she were going to have one, I think it would be great if she had a miniature version of what I've got on my back at the bottom of her spine.

The day Brooklyn was born was the most memorable day of my life, but I'll always remember the day Victoria and I got married, too. It was an amazing occasion for both of us. The day went very quickly, but the important thing was that Victoria and I spent every minute of our time together and that's what made it so special. We did spend a lot of time making sure everyone else was okay, but we were very aware that it was our day and we should try to appreciate every moment.

We both agreed that we didn't really want a stag or hen night. We're not into that sort of thing. Obviously a stag night doesn't have to involve strippers and total drunkenness, but I think with the type of people we've got around us that it would probably have ended up like that. Instead, the night before the wedding we had a big dinner with all our family and friends, the best man and the bridesmaids. Afterwards, at about half past eleven, I took Victoria down the walkway towards the tents, with a bottle of champagne and two glasses, and we sat there for a while with Brooklyn. It was just starting to rain but it was quite warm and we sat looking at the stars. At midnight, Victoria went her way and I went mine. She went in with Brooklyn and I stayed downstairs and played snooker and had a few drinks with my dad and all the men.

Victoria was staying upstairs with her sister and mum. I had to stay downstairs in the cold bit of the castle and Victoria had the nice warm luxurious bit upstairs because she is a princess! I did try to sneak up, but I didn't get into her room to see her in the end, so I had no idea at all what her dress was going to be like.

I wasn't nervous about getting married but I was nervous about the occasion. There was no need for me to be worried about whether Victoria was going to turn up or not because we were so much in love that there was no chance of her standing me up. I thought it would all go smoothly but it was a big day, so I did have a few shaky moments.

I was very nervous about the speeches. I wanted to thank everyone and express my feelings, not just to Victoria who knew them already, but to let everyone who was there know how I felt about Victoria. I had a couple of drinks before I got up to speak but I wasn't over the limit. I hadn't written the speech until the night before the wedding and as it turned out, I didn't even look at what I'd written while I was speaking. I didn't need to, especially when I spoke about Victoria. I felt very shaky when I started but it was okay in the end. I was surprised that my speech went on for over ten minutes.

We had a big wedding because it's such a special day when you get married. We both wanted it like that, not just for us, but for our mums and dads. There weren't any embarrassing moments during the day, although I got very hot in the folly, where the ceremony was held. I remember someone passing me a tissue because I was very sweaty and looked like I was going to pass out. And I cried when Victoria came into the folly. She looked unbelievable, really gorgeous. The dress was fantastic, even though she had to change out of it later because she couldn't breathe.

We went to the South of France on our honeymoon but unfortunately we had to come back after five days because the manager wanted me back in training early, which was a bit of a disappointment. Still, it was the start of something special and being married felt very different from being boyfriend and girlfriend. It was great to get away together, with the wedding rings on our fingers, and look back at the wedding photos and all the lovely things people said about us on the day. Brooklyn came with us, of course. He goes everywhere with us.

People often ask us why we haven't got a nanny for Brooklyn and the answer is because we've got two in our mums. We've said from day one that we don't want a nanny. We want to be in control of Brooklyn ourselves. We've noticed with people who have nannies that when the child falls over or something, instead of running to the mum and dad they will run to the nanny. We never want that to happen, so when we were talking about having kids, we decided not to have a nanny. Luckily, our parents absolutely love children and are very much involved in helping us look after him.

My parents were strict. They were probably stricter than I'll be with Brooklyn and our kids, although we are fairly strict with him. He won't get away with a lot of things and we are trying our best not to spoil him. Well, maybe that's unavoidable but he'll be treated pretty much like Victoria and I were when we were young.

Victoria and I are both very close to our families and think it is very important that Brooklyn sees a lot of them as well. I'm more like my mum than my dad, although there are aspects of my dad in me that come out at certain times. I'm stubborn like my dad, but he's quite hard-faced and can be sarcastic. He says things that I wouldn't say. Although I know he's joking, he sometimes says things to people and I think, you shouldn't have said that. But he doesn't see anything wrong with it so that's that, he's right. It's quite hard to upset him.

My mum will just get on with it and agree with him. She's quite soft, like me. I still hug my mum and dad, even now. I suppose it must be quite unusual because I've never seen any of my friends do it, although Victoria's like that with her mum and dad as well. Victoria's unbelievably similar to her own dad. She can be quite stubborn, like my dad and me, and she's also fiery, like my dad. He gets fired up very easily. If something is said about me, my dad will want to punch whoever said it but if my mum hears it, she'll just want to cry.

I'm terribly stubborn, which isn't a good thing. When I think I'm right, I won't budge. I do occasionally admit I'm wrong but even then I always think, well, if that hadn't happened, then I wouldn't have done whatever it was. I can always see a way round it. The quality I least like in myself is my short temper. I think I got it from my dad, but thankfully it never comes out with Brooklyn or Victoria.

I liked Victoria's parents, Jackie and Tony, as soon as I met them, although I don't think they were quite sure about me at first. The thought of their daughter going out with a footballer didn't appeal because of the reputation footballers have, but I get on really well with both of them now. In the beginning, they didn't have a clue who I was and knew nothing about football. Jackie moans now because Tony will often sit in the lounge and put football on, whereas three or four years ago, he wasn't interested. She blames me for turning him into a fan. Tony really seems to enjoy football now and he comes to games whenever he can. These days he gets nearly as annoyed as my dad does when someone kicks me or people say things about me.

I also get on very well with Christian and Louise, Victoria's brother and sister. Christian is pretty laid back and doesn't really care what's going on around him. He just gets on with his life and enjoys what he does. He's a nice person and I enjoy playing golf with him. We're on about the same level so we have good games together. Louise is the total opposite to Christian. She's more outgoing and loud and always on the go, wanting to do things and to be out all the time. She's really good fun.

Victoria and I get on very well with each other's families but I spend more time at her parents' house than she does at mine. It's very relaxed at my in-laws' house. There's a lot of coming and going and things going on, whereas at my mum's, it's an organised thing. You'll know that someone's coming round at two o'clock and we'll have lunch and that'll be it. At Jackie's, it's a question of eat when you can and get a word in when you can. It's nutty and great and I enjoy it.

I found it hard to strike a balance between being married with a baby and being my mum and dad's little boy. It's been difficult getting away from that and establishing a new identity because my mum and dad are used to being totally involved in everything I do and spending so much time with me. That isn't possible in the same way now that I have a life with Victoria and Brooklyn. They have to come first. I think my parents found that hard, particularly to begin with, which I can understand.

I suppose I would have had to become more independent even if I hadn't got married when I did. My dad has always loved football and although my mum only got into it when I did, now it's their life. Even when I'm not playing, they'll go and watch the Man United game. They worship Man United. It's a problem at times because occasionally, like with any job, I don't get on with some of the things that go on at the club and they say, 'Well, it's Man United.' Now I mainly talk to Victoria who knows all about what goes on there.

Victoria and I always turn to each other first if we have any problems and that is how it should be. I don't know that much about Victoria's business or what goes on with her but at the end of the day, if she's upset, then I listen and if I'm upset, she listens. With the Spice Girls, things have gone on that I couldn't get involved in and that I didn't want to get involved in, but whenever I saw Victoria upset, I would always be there if she needed me to fall back on.

I'm still close to my mum and dad. We've got the same affection and love for each other and because my mum and dad get on so well with Victoria's mum and dad, they're often at Victoria's parents' house and I get to see them there. It's so often the way in relationships that the woman revolves around her parents' house and, as a result, the boyfriend or husband does too. Since Brooklyn was born, I've realised that it's hard when you have a son because he'll meet a girl one day and they'll go off together. I think that's the way it is with boys and you just have to accept it. I don't see a lot of my mum at home these days. When I go to London, I'll pop in for half an hour but that's it. Then I'll be round Victoria's parents. With daughters it's totally different and my mum and dad see my sisters all the time. My parents don't like the fact that they don't see me much, but at the end of the day, I think they accept it as a natural progression. I admire them for the way they've come to terms with it.

We've never fallen out over that or anything else. Mum and Dad were always there for me and I know they always will be, as I am for them.

Victoria and I both have a lot of work commitments which means we spend a lot of time apart. That makes spending time together as a family, just the three of us, precious. We don't get to do it as much as we'd like to. Earlier in the year, there was a time when Victoria was working hard in Manchester and she was absolutely shattered. It was coming up to the end of the season and we'd already won the League. After one game, the manager asked how I felt about having some time off, in between certain games, before I met up with England for Euro 2000. That gave me the idea of planning a surprise holiday for us.

Without telling Victoria I had the extra time off, I made all the arrangements for the two of us and Brooklyn to go away to Tuscany, to a place we love. We don't get much hassle there and we get looked after and fed, so it's very relaxing.

Victoria has always wanted a puppy but I've told her that I think it's unfair to have one until we move into our new house. Still, whenever I say I've got a surprise for her, she always thinks it's going to be a puppy. So when I went to pick her up to go away and I said I had a surprise for her, I think she thought we were going to a dog shelter. I'd packed all our bags and sent them to the airport in a separate car, and I was wearing everyday clothes, combats and a vest.

My mum was in Manchester at the time, so as we approached the airport I said I was seeing Mum off back to London. But we didn't go to the main terminal but to the one where the private planes are parked. Victoria looked at me and said, 'Where are we going?'

I told her that the surprise was that we were going away for a relaxing holiday and all she said was, 'Oh!' I was thinking she was gutted because she was not getting a dog after all, but actually she was just very surprised. She'd been looking forward to going home, having a bath and getting into bed. She was happy though when I told her we were going to Tuscany for a week. She needed the break as much, if not more, than I did. She puts so much into her work and never does anything halfheartedly, so she can get quite tired.

A typical day on that holiday, and my idea of a perfect day, was waking up with Victoria and Brooklyn at around 10 and having bacon sandwiches for breakfast. Then we'd go for a quiet, relaxing walk. Because we've got such busy lives, it's nice to be somewhere quiet and out of the way, where all you can hear are the birds and there's no one near you. That's the kind of walk I like. We didn't go sightseeing. We rarely do when we have time off. We prefer to relax and do nothing much. After the walk, we'd drive back to where we were staying and get in the pool with Brooklyn, who's just learning to swim. He loves the water and always tries to dive in on his own. He just walks over to the pool and throws himself in without looking. He's a proper little boy. So I'd have a play with him and then he would go to sleep, leaving Victoria and me with a few hours to ourselves, to relax and chat and do whatever we wanted to do.

I'd have pasta and salad for lunch, with a glass of wine, then go back to the pool for a few hours to spend some time with Victoria and Brooklyn. Late afternoon, I'd go upstairs, have a lovely hot bath while Brooklyn's playing in the room and have a lie down before dinner. It's great to sit and chat and drink wine in the evening, and the food we had in Tuscany was the best I've ever had. We ate and drank most of the time. When you're away, there's nothing better than sitting down, having your dessert after a good meal, with a nice glass of red wine and a nice glass of white wine in front of you. It's unbeatable. I don't like watching telly on holiday and there isn't one in the place we stayed in Tuscany. We'd go to bed quite late, or just whenever we started feeling tired. That was my ideal day.

It was my birthday while we were away and Victoria was upset about that because she hadn't bought me anything. But she arranged for a couple of suits to be sent over from William Hunt, and an earring, which was lovely. She also surprised me by flying both mums and dads over for the day. I had no idea they were coming. The night before my birthday, we were upstairs and I heard a buzzer at about 11.30. The place we were in was in the middle of nowhere and Victoria was a bit nervous at night, so I said I would go down to see who it was.

She said, 'No, don't worry about it. It'll just be someone who's come to the wrong address.' I thought, the wrong address? We're in the middle of nowhere! But I just went with it. To be honest, I didn't really want to go down anyway. It's a bit of an eerie place but nice for that, because it's a good excuse to spend lots of time cuddling in bed, playing scared. I woke up in the morning, went down for breakfast and found my mum and dad and Victoria's mum and dad waiting for me. The mums had decorated one of the rooms with balloons and flowers. We all had a drink and a laugh and it was one of the best birthdays I've had.

The holiday was great but Victoria still wants her puppy. We've already got two Rottweilers, Puffy and Snoopy, and they're looking after the house in Hertfordshire at the moment. We haven't bought Brooklyn any pets yet because he's too young but we may get him one when he's older. I know it won't be a cat because I don't know why but I really hate cats. Maybe we'll get him a rabbit. We had about five rabbits when I was a child and I loved them. I used to have a dummy and one day my mum told me that the rabbits had eaten it, so that she could get me out of the habit of sucking it. I was gutted and cried for days but it didn't put me off the rabbits. Once we move into the house, we'll have all the space we need for animals. We've got planning permission for ten stables so we might keep horses at some time in the future but there are a lot of things to sort out with the house first.

We were looking for a family house in London for quite a while before we found the house the press call 'Beckingham Palace'. As soon as we drove through the gates, it felt right. It was absolutely perfect, exactly what we were looking for. It's a big house but you don't get lost in it and it doesn't have that ghostly, scary feeling some big houses have. It's got a homely atmosphere.

We've both got to have a place where we feel completely comfortable because we get quite a bit of hassle and attention when we're out in public. It's important to have somewhere we can go to relax and feel safe. We've got that in Manchester and with Victoria's mum and dad, but we wanted somewhere of our own near London as well. We've got candles all over the apartment in Manchester and we've had many nights sitting on our big, comfy settee, with all the candles alight, watching a film. That's my idea of heaven. Although we're looking forward to our house being finished, because of my commitment to Manchester United we won't be spending all our time there and intend to keep our home in Manchester as well.

Victoria's had most of the input as far as designing the new house and organising everything is concerned. She loves doing that sort of thing. The only rooms I've designed are the snooker room, which is where all my trophies, medals and shirts will go, and the gym. I've left the rest to Victoria because she's got a great eye. She has also had more time to go around looking at things. I've seen all the designs and what she's chosen and it's all beautiful.

I absolutely loved Christmas as a child, and I still do, so I'm really looking forward to having Christmas in our new house if I have a day off. When I was a child, the night before Christmas my mum would give us a bath early so we were all washed and ready for bed when my dad got home from work at about 6 p.m. with a family box of Kentucky Fried Chicken. Then we'd all sit and watch the Christmas movie, films like *Someone's Nicked The Dinosaur* or something like that. After the film, we'd get the food ready for the reindeer and Santa, and then we'd all go to bed. I never used to stay up to try to see Santa. I just wanted to go to bed and sleep so that the morning would come quicker.

I used to get good presents. Scalectrix was one of my favourites. I remember one year Lynne and I got a silver bike each and that was one of my best presents ever. There was a lady who always used to buy us the most horrendous presents. We'd have to go to her house every year and thank her and be nice to her. At least we learnt that it's the thought that counts at the end of the day!

Brooklyn's first Christmas was great. After he'd unwrapped everything, he was more interested in the packaging than anything else. His favourite toy was a red sports car, a big Jaguar. It's battery operated and whenever he presses the pedal, it moves along and he makes car noises.

We've talked about having Brooklyn christened after we've moved into our new house and having a big party to celebrate. I'm not religious. I don't go to church or pray, but I have a sense of spirituality and I definitely want Brooklyn to be christened. I'm actually a quarter Jewish. My mum's dad is Jewish and I've probably had more contact with Judaism than any other religion. I wore skull caps when I was younger and went to Jewish weddings with my grandad. I'm not sure if I believe in life after death. I haven't made my mind up yet.

It made me laugh when I read about the golden Buddha image of me in Thailand. It's obviously something serious over there and I feel very honoured but when I saw it in the paper, the headline said something like, Now Beckham is a God! I stuck it up in Victoria's parents' house and told everyone to bow to it when they went past. You have to laugh about something like that and although it is an honour that people think of me in that way it feels a bit weird. I would like to go to see the statue if I had the chance. The only thing is it probably would have looked better to Buddhists with my shaven head, but instead it's got the old style.

CHAPTER 4
WORLD CUP TROUBLES

I met Glenn Hoddle for the first time when he came over to the Toulon tournament in France when I was there with the England Under-21s. It was the summer of Euro '96, just before he took over the job from Terry Venables and at that point he was one of my heroes. He had been a great technical player and a brilliant passer of the ball so for someone like me, he was an obvious person to look up to. He came out to Toulon to see a few people but he didn't say much to me. There was a story that I had my England Under-21 shirt signed by him but it wasn't true.

He gave me my first England cap in his first game as manager. I had been playing well for United but I was still surprised to be called up for the World Cup qualifier in Moldova in September 1996. Alex Ferguson said to me one day, 'I think he's going to pick you,' but I didn't hear anything until it was formally announced. It was an amazing feeling at 21. I would be lying if I said I hadn't thought about it, but you don't dare to get your hopes up too much.

The first time I really spoke to him was when I turned up with England that first time. I was terrified, to be honest, but I was lucky that Gary Neville was in the squad and he was used to it. We travelled down together so I wouldn't have to walk into the Burnham Beeches hotel on my own. I was bloody nervous because there were all these big players there, including Paul Gascoigne and Stuart Pearce. I didn't know them and I wasn't sure what the reception would be. It was made worse by the fact that I have always found going away on trips with club or country hard. I like to stay close to my friends and family. I was going out with Victoria by then and it was hard leaving her. It is even worse now that I have to leave Brooklyn as well. I spoke to Victoria a lot on that first trip because I was nervous and as usual chalked up a huge bill on the hotel telephone.

There was no chance of us going out shopping or sightseeing in Moldova. I had to look it up on the map before we went. On those foreign trips you only ever get to see airports, hotels and training grounds. If you are somewhere glamorous it can get frustrating. A lot of the time you are just hanging around the hotel.

The good news was that I knew before we went that I would be making my debut. At the end of our first training session at Bisham Abbey, the manager had taken me to one side and told me I would be playing out on the right. I suppose he wanted to settle any nerves and give me a few days to get used to what I was going to have to do. I did appreciate that and it definitely helped me to prepare.

I thought I did quite well in Moldova and I was the only player to take part in every one of the World Cup matches that took us to France '98. I played some wide on the right and some in the middle of midfield and I felt I fitted pretty well into international football. The game in Rome when we qualified for the World Cup was one of the best nights of my career so far. The build-up was strange because I had been suffering from a slight cold and the manager decided to play some mind games with the Italian camp by making out that it was worse than it was. The manager told me not to come out training even though I could, just to confuse them. It was a bit weird but if it gave us an advantage then I was happy to go along with it.

I was pretty confident I would be going to the World Cup because I had played in all the qualifying games, but everyone gets nervous when the squad is announced. You worry for your mates as well as for yourself. People who think they might miss out get tense and that can spread among the rest of the players. Kevin Keegan dealt with that as well as anyone could when he had to do it just before the last European Championship. He marked people's cards and, when the time came, he made a point of going to the players' rooms as soon as he could so that they weren't pacing around all day waiting for the news.

Hoddle did it differently and in my opinion it was totally wrong. We were out at the golf resort in La Manga in Spain. Everyone had an appointment to see him in his room. I remember when it was my turn, I went along and there was Gary Neville outside. It was like a waiting room. That just made it worse. My meeting went smoothly. I was only in there for a couple of minutes and Hoddle just said, 'Obviously you are in and it's going to be a great tournament for you. You just have to concentrate.' But it still felt a terrible day. It was tough for all the United lads because Nicky Butt and Phil Neville were left out. We are all like brothers so it hit us pretty bad. It was particularly gutting for Phil because he had been told a couple of days earlier that he had no worries.

The lads had played golf in the morning but when the meetings started there was still no gossip that Gazza might be dropped. I had been by the pool with him just before he went in to see the manager and he had been saying how much he was looking forward to the tournament. The night before there had been a players' social evening and we had all had a drink. We were all jollied up and enjoying ourselves. It was a closed bar in the hotel so it was not as if there was going to be any problem with the press or public. There was karaoke going on and Gazza was the star of the show because he loves performing on a stage but he was not the only one getting stuck in. FA staff including Terry Byrne and Steve Slattery, the masseurs, were there too and we were all laughing and joking. It was exactly the sort of night you need before a big tournament and the sort of occasion when Gazza is at his best.

It is amazing to look back and think he was about to be dropped and I must say I thought it was wrong to leave Gazza out of the World Cup. If the manager was worried about his drinking, I am sure he could have handled it in a way that would have been good for everyone, including the team. I don't think there was a player in the squad who didn't think that Gazza should come, even if it was just to contribute 30 minutes in matches. He is that good a player that, in a tournament like the World Cup, you might need him just to come on and turn a game around in a little burst when things are tight. I'm sure he would have been able to handle coming off the bench instead of starting.

Gazza is a great guy and very popular with the players. Once he gets to know you, there is no more generous bloke around. If he had been handled sensitively, I am sure he could have coped with the tournament. Everyone is different and needs treating differently but Gazza did not get that. I was gutted for him when he was left out and I was not the only one.

Leaving him out gave all the players a big shock but I think it was the way the manager did it that caused the biggest problems. It affected the mood among the rest of the players. We were still talking about it in the weeks that followed, what a big decision it was, but also what damage it must have done to a mate.

What Hoddle came out with in his World Cup diary about Gazza trashing his hotel room that day just made it worse. There is a privacy and trust between managers and players which should always be there. That is why the bond at United is so strong because we know that if there are big rows between people, all the details won't get out into the public arena. People can be honest with each other. Whatever went on in that room should have been a private matter.

I never read Hoddle's book, just the bits and bobs that were serialised, including that rubbish about me not being focused. Apparently, other things in the book were completely out of order and all the senior players were angry. I am not sure if anything was said to the manager's face but I think he knew our feelings. We lost respect for him over that but I think what happened with Gazza in La Manga started the problems.

All the stuff about Eileen Drewery, the faith healer, didn't help the manager either. I saw her once and I have got nothing against her as a person. People can believe what they like, but I have never been into that type of thing. That did not stop the manager coming up to me before the World Cup and saying it might be good for me to see her. She had a room at Burnham Beeches where the players would visit her and he gave me an appointment time. I am not sure what good he thought it would do. Maybe he thought it would help with the temper problem he was making such a big deal about.

I went in and she stuck her hands on my head and on my face. We just chatted about things but I didn't feel any sensations except that her hands were really warm. It was only for 15 minutes or so. There was a lot of joking about it among the players and then that story came out about Ray Parlour asking her for a short back and sides. I wasn't angry about seeing her but it felt like an obligation, which wasn't right. It felt like you had to see her or the manager would hold it against you, which isn't the way to treat players.

Although the players were unhappy about Gazza being left out and there was all the talk about Eileen Drewery in the press, coming up to the World Cup I was focused. I was ready to play. It was the biggest competition I had ever been involved in so I would hardly be in any other state of mind. It was the World Cup. There is no player in the world who won't be focused. Unfortunately, the manager saw it differently.

I've got so many mixed memories from the World Cup. It started badly, then it suddenly went great and everyone knows what happened in the end. I wasn't at all happy at the beginning. I had not had many disappointments in my career at that stage. In fact, I had hardly suffered any, which made it even worse when I found out that I was not going to start the biggest tournament of my life.

I had played in every game leading up to the tournament and I had no reason at all to think that the manager would not pick me for the first game against Tunisia in Marseilles. I was really looking forward to it. We were out on the training pitch a few days before the match and he announced the team. I wasn't in it. I thought he might have pulled me to the side beforehand to break the news but I just had to stand there with the other players and take it.

There had been no warning or explanation. Instead he asked me to go straight in and do a big press conference. He had said beforehand that if you weren't in the team, you would still have to see the press but I wasn't happy having to go and put a brave face on it. I'm not very good at hiding my feelings so it was very hard for me that day. The team had an important game coming up so I did my best not to show my hurt to the rest of the lads. But it wasn't easy. I was in Gary's room a lot and on the phone ringing my mum and dad and Victoria. Gary was the person I was really talking to because he is great at offering advice.

I went to see the manager before the game and asked him why I had been left out. He said I wasn't focused and that my mind was elsewhere. I don't know if that was just an excuse because he had different ideas about the team but, in my mind, it was ridiculous. It was the World Cup. I had been thinking about that since I was a kid. I told him I didn't agree with him. I really don't know what was going through his mind. I thought I deserved to play and the other lads were supportive. There was a rumour that he was not happy with my performance when we had played a match against a local club team behind closed doors in France, but no one said anything. That game had gone okay. We had won and nothing was said about how I played.

We did get some impression that keeping Michael Owen and me on the sidelines was creating headlines at home but we couldn't be certain because we weren't allowed to read any papers. They were all banned by the manager. I don't read a lot of them anyway but it is sometimes good to see what the mood is about things and your family and friends will tell you anyway in the end.

Leaving me out came totally out of the blue but I just had to get on with it. Dad and Victoria said that when I got my chance I had to make the most of it. Gary was great and I got support from Tony Adams and David Seaman but I was gutted. I am a professional and you learn to pick yourself up but it was tough. It is important to feel that you can trust the manager but I was moping around the hotel not knowing what was happening or where I stood. I was devastated not to be playing. My pride took a bit of a battering that week. I wanted to be involved and no one could give me a good reason why I was left out. I am not shifting the blame for the sending off against Argentina on to the manager but I do believe that it was all the frustration of those early days coming out.

I missed the 2-0 victory against Tunisia when Alan Shearer and Paul Scholes scored and I didn't start against Romania either. It was obvious that, with the team winning, he would not change the side but it was a very frustrating night in Toulouse. The England fans got a bit jittery when we went behind. I eventually came on when Paul Ince got injured and I thought I did well. Michael Owen came on and equalised for us and, even though we lost 2-1 when Dan Petrescu scored in the last minute, I thought things were fitting into place.

The players were all confident that we could beat Colombia in the last group game and go on to the next round. It all worked to plan in Lens and my free kick in the 2-0 win over Colombia was one of my favourites. The manager had told me to have a go whenever I thought I was close enough. It was quite far out and I'm sure a few of the players were wondering if it was worth it, but sometimes you have to go with your gut instincts. I just felt right for that one and it curved and dipped in.

That goal will always be special to me, not because of the finish from far out or the fact that it was my first goal for England but because it came in the World Cup finals. It had been my dream since I was a kid to score at the World Cup. I'm sure it's the same for every football-mad kid. To do it with a goal like that was unbelievable.

I thought things had turned around at last but even after we had beaten Colombia there was a problem between the manager and me. It came in training the morning after that victory and it was made worse because I had not got to sleep until at least 3 a.m. I always find it hard to fall asleep after a big match and I was even more excited than usual after scoring that goal. So I had had only a few hours proper rest and I had not done any stretching when the manager asked me to take a free kick. Incey was still injured so I think it was Paul Scholes flicking balls up to me. I lobbed it over the wall instead of whacking it because I was still warming up. It was from the same place that I had scored the night before but the manager came up and said in front of everybody, 'Obviously you haven't got the ability to do that.' He did apologise afterwards but you could see all the other lads were wondering what was going on.

At least we were through to the next stage, the goals were going in and I felt on a high. Not all the players were happy with the manager but as a professional you get on with it. We were through to face Argentina in St Etienne in the last 16 and I was really up for the game.

The first half in St Etienne went well. There were the two penalties to make it 1-1 and then I played a little ball through to send Michael away on his wonder goal. With someone of his ability and with his pace, you just give them the pass and let them get on with it. It was a fantastic goal and even better for him because, like me, he had been frustrated by being kept on the bench at the start of the tournament. When Argentina equalised just before half-time to make it 2-2, it was a big blow because we had been getting on top of them and they had had just a couple of chances.

As well as all the goals, there were a few physical things going on, just a few nicks in the first half. Diego Simeone is a difficult player to come up against, someone who always makes it tough, and he was trying to put me off. He always has a little tug or says things. You have got to try to ignore that and I didn't feel particularly wound up, but maybe the frustration was rising.

I didn't think I needed to watch my temperament at the time but it kept coming up in the press and I don't think the manager helped me. People kept asking him about it but whereas at United we keep those things in-house, he kept talking about it. That kept the thing going and blew it out of proportion.

He always seemed to be critical, which gave people a chance to write about it and that didn't help. If everyone is going on about something, then it is bound to be in your mind. Alex Ferguson always stands up for his players. That is one of the reasons why we win things, even with a lot of young players. He never slaughters us in public.

Whether I was frustrated or not, all I remember is that the ball was played up to me and I felt a shove in the back. Then I think the ball hit me in the face or chest and I felt a slap on the head or as if my hair was pulled and Simeone said something. If I had not lifted my right leg nothing would have happened and, to this day, I am convinced I hardly touched him. But I just flicked my foot up instinctively, he went down and that was the start of it all.

It is hard talking about it even now. Gary Neville came up to me as soon as it happened and said, 'What did you do that for?' I think he knew by the expression on the referee's face what was coming but I didn't expect the red at all. I honestly thought I had hardly done anything but after he booked Simeone, I realised what was coming. Out came the red card.

When I walked off I was in a bit of a daze. I walked straight past the manager who didn't say anything to me and down the tunnel into the dressing room. I stayed down there until extra time and penalties when I came out again to watch. I was with Terry Byrne who took me in. We ended up in the drug-testing room watching the rest of normal time on the TV. We weren't saying much. We were trying to make sense of it all. I remember him saying, 'It must have happened for a reason.' I went into the shower at one point and Terry ran in and said, 'Sol has scored.' I was delighted but then he ran back saying it had been disallowed for a foul.

Before extra time started, I went to phone Victoria. She had seen it all from where she was on tour in the United States. They were filming a Spice Girls documentary at the time and she was in an English bar with Mel C and her mum and dad. The camera was actually on her when it all happened. I don't think she could make sense of it at the time and when we spoke she was just asking what happened. I couldn't tell her because I still couldn't get my head round it myself.

After the penalties that put us out of the World Cup, I went back into the dressing room as the rest of the players came back in. They were obviously all totally gutted and most of them just slumped down. The only person who came and spoke to me then was Tony Adams. I needed it at that point. I was on the opposite side of the dressing room from him, just sitting on my own in my tracksuit and he came up and said, 'Don't you ever think you have ever let us down. You're a great player and I love you to bits.' It meant a lot to me and I will always remember it. It especially meant a lot because everyone knows what Tony has been through, how he has handled himself and what he's achieved. He's got perspective in his life so for him to come up and say what he did was brilliant. Apart from that, nothing was said. I was sitting next to Alan Shearer and I just said, 'Sorry.' That was it. There wasn't a lot more I could say and most of the players were in their own worlds.

I went through every emotion. I did get angry in the changing room, with myself and with the whole situation for a while but when we went to leave I felt numb. It was only when I saw my mum and dad as we were leaving the ground that I cracked up. That was rock bottom because the whole experience hit me. I am quite an emotional person. I cried watching the film *Armageddon* and I get a lump in my throat just watching some reunion on a show like *Surprise, Surprise*. But I had not cried like I did then since I was a child. For a good 10 minutes, I just lost it. I didn't cry anything like that again until I heard I was going to be a dad.

People said I should have come out and spoken to the press immediately but I couldn't sit in front of cameras at a time like that. I would have felt on trial. Certain people were pushing me to say something but I thought it would make things worse. I know some people interpreted that as me not caring but that was not the case. I didn't want to let go in front of people and I was feeling very emotional.

I kept my head down and went straight past all the television crews and reporters and got on the coach next to Gary. It was a quiet journey back to our base in La Baule and when we got back to the team hotel, I had a few drinks and played pool late into the night with a couple of the backroom staff. The next morning we flew back to England and I was still feeling pretty numb. The manager pulled me on the plane and we stood in the middle. He said it was one of those things and I had to learn from it. I didn't say much back to him. I was still coming to terms with it.

I got a few calls from people and one of the first messages was from Alex Ferguson. He just told me, 'It's in the past. Get back to Manchester where people love you and get playing football again.' I really appreciated the message but I needed to get away and I wanted to see Victoria, so I caught a plane to New York within hours of landing back in London. My parents were waiting at the Heathrow terminal for me in a private room. They were already starting to bear the brunt of all the attention with the press camped outside their house. I got some clothes from them and headed off to the States.

I know I've not always been an angel. There are things I have done that I have regretted but there were times after the World Cup when I was treated like a criminal. It was probably even worse for my parents who didn't deserve any of the nightmare that came after the sending off. They suffered more than anybody.

I don't think I have ever gone around trying to get opponents sent off, which makes it annoying that Simeone got off scot free after the Argentina game. I have seen him since the World Cup when United played against Inter Milan in the Champions League. People made so much out of the reunion but nothing was going to happen. I wasn't going to be so stupid as to get sent off again and we ended up swapping shirts. Some people said we had kissed and made up but, to be honest, that has not happened. Some players try to get others sent off and I think he made it a lot worse for me. That happens more and more in football these days. It seems to be part of the game.

When I went away to America after the World Cup, I managed to ignore almost everything that was going on back in England. My parents protected me from it all. It was they who were bearing the brunt of it. At one point they were sure their phone was being tapped because there were things they were saying which were getting out and it couldn't be coincidence. My mum would turn up at places and there would be photographers already there waiting for her at exactly the right time. She is a hairdresser and mostly works in old people's homes. She only does it occasionally but the press seemed to know exactly where she was going and when. There were all the abusive phone calls as well. They thought about changing their home number but they couldn't because my dad uses it for work.

All this horrendous stuff was going on but I didn't know much about it over in the States. When I came back I saw a few newspaper clippings but the last thing I wanted to do was go over it all. There were some things I couldn't avoid. When I came back there was a television documentary, *The Trouble with Beckham*. It was such rubbish that they had to get a load of West Ham fans on just to slag me off. At the end of the film, I bet everyone was thinking, 'What is the trouble with Beckham?' I had been sent off once in my life which hardly put me among the bad boys of football.

There were times when I stepped back from it and thought everything had gone mad. But mostly I just tried to keep my head down and get on with my job and my life. As soon as I got back to training, the manager called me into his office and we talked about what had gone on. I already knew he would be supportive because he had been among the first to call me after I was sent off. He had also come out publicly and criticised Glenn Hoddle for putting me in a press conference in France after I was dropped. That also meant a lot to me. I heard about it from my dad and it helped me through a bad time.

The manager told me to ignore all the criticism that was coming my way but I did take note of some of the people who slaughtered me after Argentina. I've got a little book in which I've written down the names of those people who upset me the most. I don't want to name them because I want it to be a surprise when I get them back. I know I will get them some day.

Most people were supportive to my face and I didn't get a lot of stick on the pitch. I think there is a convention among players that they won't kick a guy when he's down, although you will always get some who will. The one I most remember is Mauricio Tarrico at Spurs. I had no reason to expect anything from him at all but I remember him having a go. Maybe it was because he is Argentinian but he was being really mouthy. Strangely, he didn't play up at Old Trafford for Spurs in the return game that season. Maybe he was scared and was expecting something back.

Generally opponents treated me fine and I was pleased to be back playing. Even though we lost the Charity Shield 3-0 to Arsenal in my first game back, I was surrounded by my mates and the United fans were so behind me it was brilliant. We went to Upton Park for one of the first games of the season and I think it was good to get that out of the way early on. Paul Ince always got terrible stick when he went to West Ham because he had played there earlier in his career, but my reception made the reactions to Incey look pretty mild. Luckily I didn't have a bad game and it wasn't the sort of match with loads of dodgy tackles flying. On the pitch it wasn't bad at all. It was only when I got to the touchline that it became horrendous. People were standing up, swearing, spitting and throwing things at me. They still do.

Sometimes it could be quite funny. I have been hit by thongs and knickers, especially after Victoria came out with that joke about me trying on her clothes. If you see the interview it is obvious she was just making a joke. You try to lighten up with people and it still gets twisted round. After what she said, a bloke stood up at Derby County and threw a thong at me. The police picked it up and took it away. I didn't want to touch it in case it had been worn.

A lot of the stick was much worse than that, and that is when it gets really upsetting. I used to hate the songs about Victoria when they first started but after a while you get used to them. You brush them off. What I will never accept is songs about Brooklyn. I think anyone is entitled to stick up for their children.

I knew I would get stick after the World Cup but I cannot believe how long it has gone on. There must be a lot of jealous people out there. Every time I think it has disappeared, I know I will meet some idiot who will have a go at me. Sometimes it is at matches, sometimes just driving down the road.

Maybe I dress differently at times but that is not a crime. I get all this stuff thrown at me but I don't think I have let myself down at all as a professional footballer and I want to be well respected as a player. All the stick I get seems to stretch back to the Argentina game and I don't think it will ever end. I just get on with my life and enjoy it. I have always enjoyed it and I don't think I've got anything to regret. Obviously it is not something I am proud of but, in a way, it has had a positive effect with all the support I've had. Victoria, my family and friends, and Alex Ferguson stood by me at a difficult time and you don't ever forget that. I found out who my true friends and allies are.

CHAPTER 5
WINNING WAYS

I don't think anything will ever match that treble season of 1998-99. I will spend the rest of my career trying to equal it. If I could win the World Cup with England, that would be the ultimate but I think the treble will be hard to cap. With so many games for club and country, it gets harder and harder to win more than one trophy in a season.

At United, we set off with the intention of winning something each season. You have priorities but the most important thing is to pick up some silverware to keep the fans happy. So many things can upset your plans. You can get injuries and suspensions or it can just be a change of luck. Anything can happen. I think the treble turned on the FA Cup semi-final against Arsenal when we won 2-1 at Villa Park after extra time. If Peter Schmeichel had not saved that penalty from Dennis Bergkamp right at the end of 90 minutes, we would have been out and who knows what difference it would have made to Arsenal's confidence and ours. A whole season comes down to moments like that and you hope that you have the players on your team with the ability to make the difference. Luckily at United, we usually have.

The hero everyone will remember from that night is Ryan Giggs. He deserves it because his goal was one of the greatest I have seen. It was late into a hard game and everyone was getting tired but he picked the ball up and sprinted 50 yards through the Arsenal defence. People will be talking about it for years, especially because it was such an important match. Everyone will remember his celebrations when he took his shirt off and sprinted around the pitch like a madman. He got some serious stick for that from the rest of the players, mostly because of his hairy chest.

The way it all worked out was amazing. First we won the League, which is very satisfying because it is reward for a whole season. It would have been a great year even if that was all we had won. Arsenal had taken it from us the year before and we were desperate to get it back. It is nice to win it with a bit to spare, but there is a great thrill doing it on the last day of the season. We knew that if we beat Tottenham we would win the title. We had to come from behind but I scored the equaliser and then Andy Cole got the winner. We had a celebration but we didn't want to do anything that might harm our chances of winning all three trophies.

Having the title in the bag set us up in a great mood for the two Cup finals. The FA Cup is always a special day out. People have been knocking it and saying it is devalued because we didn't defend the trophy when we went to the World Club Championship in Brazil. But any player will tell you that you can't beat walking out at Wembley. It is a unique occasion.

I enjoyed the Cup final. We beat Newcastle United 2-0 with goals from Teddy Sheringham and Paul Scholes and we were always in control once Teddy scored in the 11th minute. It was hard for Roy Keane going off with an injury early in the game. He already knew that he would not be playing in the European Cup final because of suspension so that was his last game of the season. It meant that I could move into central midfield. I think I had a good game there, which might have helped the manager to make up his mind what to do when we took on Bayern Munich five days later.

It probably doesn't need saying that Barcelona was one of the great nights of my life, climaxing an unbelievable year. Everyone knows what an obsession the European Cup had become at Old Trafford. People say it was the manager's Holy Grail but I think it had spread to everyone. All the players know the history of the club and about the great triumph in 1968 with George Best and Bobby Charlton, and we always knew that we would have to win the European Cup one day to prove that we were a great team.

The best thing was the way we went over and took control against foreign teams — Inter Milan in the quarter-final and Juventus in the semi. For so many years English teams had been losing out to Italians and Germans. We hadn't been able to make an impression or come away with anything. That year we proved to foreign teams and to English clubs that it could be done. I think it gave the whole country more confidence.

We had lost to Borussia Dortmund in the semi-final two years before, which was a massive disappointment because we had about 20 chances in both games and should have got to the final. The luck just didn't seem with us then or against Monaco when we lost the next year in the quarters.

I suppose people will say we got enough luck when we won it in 1999, but I think we earned it.

Against Juventus in the semi, to come back from 2-0 down in Turin was tough but we knew we were playing well and we thought we could do it. We knew we would create chances and it was just a question of taking them. To come away from there with a 3-2 win showed the character that we had developed since we were young kids. When you grow up being told you must never stop trying, that you have to give your best to the end, it comes out at times like that. I remember being told that the minute I came to United. You get it from the youth coaches down.

The only disappointment on that night was the booking of Roy Keane and Paul Scholes which meant they were out of the final. We knew what the situation was with bookings and discipline before the match but they are the type of players who are never going to pull out of anything. Their attitude is to give it their all in every game. It showed their character the way they carried on playing after the bookings. I remember Gazza crying at the 1990 World Cup when he thought he would miss the final and I could understand that because I can be terrible at hiding my feelings. Keano and Scholesy aren't like that and they just got on with the job of getting us to the final.

That night in the Nou Camp was the greatest feeling I have known on a football pitch. The preparation could not have been better and I went out to play the final on a high. We had already won the League and the FA Cup and the day before the European Cup final, the manager told me I was playing centre midfield as I had done for most of the FA Cup final. If I'm honest, I prefer playing in the middle. I get more options and I love being at the heart of things. So when the manager told me I was doing it in the biggest game of my career, I was totally chuffed.

There was a lot going on around the club with such a big game but I was completely focused. I slept well the night before, but I always do. It is only after games that I can't get to sleep until 2 or 3 in the morning because I'm still buzzing. The night before we played Bayern Munich I was asleep by 10.30 and we weren't up till 11 the next morning. We were staying out in Sitges, a beautiful area along the coast from Barcelona, and we went for a stroll down the seafront the next day. The manager made sure there were no changes from our usual routine to keep everyone relaxed. There was the usual pre-match meal and another sleep in the afternoon for a few hours. The only thing that was different was the Versace suits I had sorted out for all the lads. I knew someone at the company and I got the whole team kitted out in some great clothes.

The manager was brave from the start. It would have been easy to pack the midfield but he wanted to go out and win the game so he picked two wingers, Giggs and Jesper Blomqvist, and put me in the middle.

For 90 minutes it was all a bit of a nightmare, even though I thought I was playing pretty well. Bayern were winning 1-0 with an early free kick, they hit the post twice and anyone would have thought it was all over. When I looked up and saw the big clock showing one minute I was convinced that was it. I don't remember much apart from how gutted I was feeling. It was one of the worst moments I had experienced on a football pitch. I even saw the trophy up in the stands with Bayern Munich ribbons already on it. It was an unbelievable sight. I was almost sick.

The way we had been brought up, I knew we couldn't just stop, so I hit a ball from middle of midfield out to Gary Neville. All I remember was him up against a blond lad who sliced it out for a corner. I ran over to take it and then I saw Peter Schmeichel charging up. I didn't think it was strange at all. It was a make or break situation and he can cause chaos when he comes up. He had scored in a European match against Rotor Volgograd before that and you could see the Germans looking around and wondering what they were going to do. Peter could be unbelievable in the air. That is why I floated the corner over instead of whipping it in like I usually do. I thought it would cause the most confusion if I aimed for Peter's head so I chipped that one up in the air. All I could see in the penalty area was Teddy Sheringham sticking his leg out and the ball going in. People ask how it feels but you are too busy trying to get on with the game.

After that goal we were flying and, looking back, I don't think it was the greatest shock ever when we pulled off the winner in injury time. You could see that the Bayern Munich players were gutted by the equaliser and we were charging forward on a high. We were just getting on with the match instead of stopping to think how lucky we were to be back in the game and that is how we won the second corner. Peter Schmeichel wasn't up for this one so I decided to whip it in as usual. I was out near the corner flag and I couldn't see everything that was going on. All I remember is Ole Gunnar Solskjaer getting his foot to it and everyone going mad. From 1-0 down with a minute to go, we were 2-1 up and the game was over.

People have said it was a victory for the English over the Germans but we just celebrated for ourselves and for the club. I felt a bit sorry for Bayern Munich, to be honest. I made sure I shook Lothar Matthaus by the hand because he was a player I had always admired and looked up to, the way he had won so much and stayed at the top for so long. I swapped shirts with him and that was a proud moment. I kept my shirt from the first half and I've got the medal and a ticket to put in a frame.

The celebrations were very emotional, especially when Keano and Scholesy came out. It was not just for show. They were a massive reason why we were through to the final in the first place. They had every right to feel as happy as we were. All the players wanted them out on the pitch and it was great when they lifted the cup in front of the fans.

I felt I had a good game that night. I kept the ball well and passed it well. I didn't need a European Cup final to prove to myself that I could play centre midfield at the highest level but it was still great to do it. It is where I can express myself best, with the range and the options and I think I showed it that night on a difficult occasion.

We were staying in the Arts Hotel in Barcelona and that night there was a great function with families, wives and girlfriends. We hadn't had the chance to celebrate winning the League or FA Cup so this was three nights rolled into one. I think I crawled to bed at 5 a.m. and I am happy to admit I was totally legless. I am not a big drinker. I have never really liked beer. I think I was drinking wine and champagne, although it is all a bit of a haze. There was loads of dancing and players singing. We flew back to Manchester at lunchtime the next day for the amazing parade in the city. We went through the city on a bus and it took hours because the streets were so packed. We realised then what winning the European Cup meant for so many people. It seemed like the whole city had been waiting for 31 years.

Now we have won the treble once, I suppose people will think we can do it again. The fact that we had to pull out of the FA Cup last year because of fixture commitments shows how long and hard the season is and the Champions League has been massively expanded. We played 13 games including a qualifying round against Lodz from Poland when we won it. Now you have to play 17 games even if you qualify automatically for the group stages. That number of games makes it hard even for the biggest clubs to field their best team all the time. I think it is possible that a team might win the treble, hopefully it will be United, and we'll certainly keep trying, but it does get harder and harder.

Winning the trophies for the club is what really matters but it is always a real honour to win individual awards and I did unbelievably on that front after the treble season. First there was the UEFA awards ceremony in Monte Carlo on the night before we played Lazio in the Super Cup. All the top coaches from the teams that had done well in Europe the previous season got to vote, so to be recognised by all those people was brilliant. Johan Cruyff was at the awards dinner and I got to chat to him for five minutes. It was fantastic to be among the big names. I had been told that I had been voted the best midfielder in Europe but I didn't know that I was going to get the main prize of the most valuable player as well. Victoria came with me and I was chuffed to bits.

Winning was great, but it meant just as much later that season to come in the top three in the European and World Player of the Year awards. To think that you are ranked the second best in the world is something that even as a kid I would not dare to hope for. I was not about to complain about not having finished first. Rivaldo has been awesome at Barcelona and he deserved the recognition.

When I was young, the wildest dreams I had were of winning the FA Cup or playing for my favourite team, Manchester United, or, when I dared, scoring in the World Cup. So for someone to say 'you're the second best footballer on the planet' is one of the greatest honours of my life. I remember my dad ringing me after it had been announced and he was nearly in tears he was so proud. Something like that really brings it home to you. I had been brought up hearing about the likes of Ruud Gullit and Maradona but I never thought I'd be up there with them.

The other thing is that it makes you want to get even better. People say to me that I should be happy with second place and of course I am. If someone had told me after the World Cup that a year later I would be voted second best player in the world and second best player in Europe, I'd have said, 'Yeah right!' But once you're second, you can't help wanting to be first. However happy you are, you want to work even harder to become the best player around and I would like to think that I have improved rather than sitting still and feeling pleased with myself.

That's something to do with my dad's influence, always pushing on to the next achievement. That's what having a competitive spirit means. You are always looking for the next challenge. I've even found myself thinking about who I would tell first if I was voted the best player. It would have to be Victoria because I am closer to her than to anyone and she has been so supportive of me over the past few years. She was so proud when I was voted second best player in the world. The next call would be to my dad. These awards were an achievement for him and Mum as well because they worked so hard when I was a kid to get me to this point in my career.

The great thing about playing in this United team is that you never get any jealousy over awards. Everyone will have been chuffed when Keano was voted Footballer of the Year last season and I think everyone was pleased for me when I got the recognition. It is easy to say, but I do think they see individual trophies as an honour for everyone. Not every team has that, which is why this United team is so special. You have either got that spirit and togetherness or you haven't and it's what kept us going in the treble season, literally to the last minute.

CHAPTER 6
EURO 2000

I was driving through central London a couple of weeks after Euro 2000 when some fans came up to the car. I had my window down and was bracing myself for the usual abuse but I couldn't have been more wrong. They came up and thanked me for trying so hard during the tournament.

For me to get a friendly greeting in London is something special, and I hope it marked a turning point in my international career. I know that there will always be some people who will abuse me, but I think what happened at Euro 2000 when my wife and son got the worst stick imaginable has made a few people stop and think. I love playing for my country and I hope I showed that in the way I performed in Holland and Belgium. It would be great to think the majority of England fans recognise that now.

I felt as relaxed as I ever have going into Euro 2000. I had come off a good season with Manchester United when we had won the championship. Even better, we had clinched it early by our standards. We have a habit of making life difficult for ourselves, but we had the title wrapped up with a few weeks to spare when we won at Southampton.

We had to wait until we played Spurs at Old Trafford a couple of weeks later before we received the trophy but, because we weren't involved in the FA Cup or the European Cup final, I had the chance to take a break in California and recharge the batteries. I knew I would be away from Victoria and Brooklyn for a few weeks so it was great to spend some good time with them. If you are relaxed in your family life, it has to help your football as well.

The preparations for the tournament went as well as could be hoped. We had a good game against Brazil when we drew 0-0 at Wembley. It was a real thrill for me to play against the most glamorous team in the world because I had been suspended when England played against them in Le Tournoi in France a few years ago. At the end, Roberto Carlos came over to me to swap shirts. He had been reported as saying some bad things about me when we played Real Madrid in the Champions League but he walked over and gave me a hug and whispered something in my ear. I think he said he had not said those things but actually I didn't understand a word.

A few days later we beat the Ukraine 2-0. The victory was spoiled a bit for me because I got some loud mouthing from a couple of idiots in the crowd but the team was getting into good shape for the tournament. We went out to Malta and even if the game wasn't too clever and we won only 2-1, it was still a good trip. My family go to Malta on holiday every year and I love it there because the people all seem to support Manchester United. It was a good trip for all the players because we had the sun on our backs and I think that always makes you feel better about life. It freshens you up. I felt better than I did going into the World Cup when Glenn Hoddle dropped me without warning. I was looking forward to it all and could not have been better prepared, physically or mentally.

The mood in the whole squad was good. Kevin Keegan was great at involving all the players and making everyone feel ready. He would sit down with us at meal times and he was always chatting away to the players. He was gentle and understanding when you needed him to be but when you needed geeing up before a match, he was the one to do it. I was missing Victoria and Brooklyn, but I felt we could go into the tournament and achieve something.

The build-up to the first game always takes forever. Hanging around a hotel the whole time can be quite hard, and different players deal with it in different ways. I played a lot of table tennis with Gary and Phil Neville and Paul Scholes. We are quite evenly matched so we have some competitive games. There was a putting green behind our hotel and the FA had brought out arcade games, pool tables and board games including Scrabble and Monopoly to keep everyone amused. I had my own portable DVD and all the latest movies. I watch the *Friends* videos all the time and I also had *Jack Frost*. There are a few films I can watch over and over again. *As Good As It Gets* with Jack Nicholson is one of them. I watched *American History X* a few times, which is a strong film.

Certain managers are happy for wives to be involved during tournaments and others don't like it. With Kevin Keegan, we didn't see them when we were away in the camp in Belgium but he tried to let us see as much of them as we could before we came out. We had a few nights at home. Our three games at

Euro 2000 were quite close together so there wasn't really time for wives and girlfriends to visit. I am sure they would have done if we had stayed longer in the competition.

Personally, I would like them to be part of it all the way through. Obviously you have a job to do, but I would love to see Victoria and Brooklyn every day when I'm at a tournament. I don't think that would affect my concentration at all. It would help it because I would not be wondering when I could speak to them or worrying if I was missing out on something at home with Brooklyn.

My job involves a lot of travel and being away from my family is one of the most difficult things. That is why Victoria flew out on a private jet to meet me when we had a spare day in the 1998 World Cup in France. All the other players wanted to play golf in La Baule but, although I quite like a round every now and then, I wanted to see Victoria. She came over and we went to a little restaurant. I couldn't see anything wrong with it but I heard afterwards that Glenn Hoddle wasn't happy. He probably thought I should have been with the lads but it is not as if we didn't spend a lot of time together anyway. I think Graeme Le Saux's wife came to visit him but no fuss was made of that. I would never miss out on anything that involves the whole team but if you are given a day off, I think you should be able to do with it what you like and seeing Victoria was my priority.

Usually I can't go out sightseeing anyway which can make the time drag. While we were in Belgium, we did visit the local town, which has a famous ancient spa. I had two baths, one in fizzy sulphurous water and the other in a bath of water jets that hit every part of the body at once, which was rather pleasant. But when I tried to go out in Tokyo on a Manchester United trip in '99, it was very busy with fans. A few of the players tried to go to the shops but we were just mobbed. You are meant to be resting but you come back even more tired than when you started.

Having a child has made it much harder because if you are away for a month, you can miss so much of their growing up. Brooklyn is a quick learner and advanced for his age so when I come back, he will be saying different things and have learnt different actions. You want to be part of all that as a dad. He is already saying 'football' and if he sees a match on the TV, he will say 'daddy' at the telly. If he recognises me on the screen, he will walk up and kiss the television. Those are priceless moments and it's hard knowing you are missing out on them.

There will always be some players who feel that, as soon as you have met up, then you are on camp and everything should be put into training. But every player is different. One of the questions I'm often asked in interviews is whether scoring a goal is better than sex. For me, there's no contest. Of course sex is better and it certainly doesn't affect my game. In my opinion, everyone should have the chance to do what suits them best. I work best when I have my family around. That has always been the case and it is even more so now that I am a husband and a dad. I can't keep my hands off Victoria anyway.

I felt great going into that first game against Portugal in Eindhoven. We knew they had some fine attacking players. I have come up against Rui Costa and Luis Figo before in the Champions League and they can both do unbelievable things. That made it even more amazing when we got off to such a flying start and were 2-0 up within 20 minutes. But even when we were racing into the lead, I was worried that they were playing through us a bit too easily.

I was chuffed to be involved in both our goals. For the first one, the marker sat off me which was quite surprising. It was almost like he was inviting me to cross so I did. Scholesy is great at taking up those positions in the box and I managed to land one on his head. Then Steve McManaman swept in a great finish after a move down the right.

At 2-0 up, maybe we got a bit carried away with it but that is how the manager likes us to play. That is how we got the lead in the first place and we thought that if we got a third it would be all over. The trouble was that we got too stretched when they started coming back at us. Paul Ince was isolated in midfield and they were running from all angles. When Luis Figo got the first with an amazing strike, I felt very uneasy and we couldn't stop their attacks.

I was gutted to lose 3-2, but some of the football we played against Portugal was the best I have been involved with for England. The manager can make you play without pressure and I enjoyed it. He liberates you. I wasn't proud, but I was chuffed that we held our own against one of the best teams around. Sometimes when you play for your country you can feel everyone getting tense. Against Portugal, the team showed the sort of attacking football that we love at United. We had lost but I was buzzing after the game and as usual after a big match I didn't get to sleep until 5 a.m.

It was disappointing to lose, but the worst thing about the night was the stick from the fans. There might not have been many fans shouting things but the ones who were gave me the worst I have ever heard, which is saying something. And it wasn't just me, it was quite a few of the players.

It started even before the game when we came out by the tunnel. Gary, Phil, me and Scholesy were getting slaughtered by some Liverpool fans. They were shouting 'Manc scum' and worse. Even when we were 2-0 up they were having a go, shouting aggressively, 'Pull your finger out, Beckham.' I had taken some abuse when we played against the Ukraine at Wembley just before the tournament when I went over to take a throw-in and a couple of blokes started shouting things at me, but this was miles worse. I was working my nuts off for my country and we were winning 2-0 and I was still getting loads of abuse. It happened again at half-time near the tunnel.

At the final whistle, I went over to clap the fans. Most of them had been amazing, getting behind the players and singing even when we were losing but then I saw a load in the stand making gestures at me and shouting disgusting abuse. That is when I flicked my finger up at them. I thought, I've been trying my hardest and that's all the thanks I get. I felt I had played well but that shouldn't matter. You shouldn't get stick like that when you are representing your country, however badly you play.

When I was walking off at the end was the worst. To be honest, I am used to all the stuff about Victoria. It was hard to take at first and I still hate it, but most of it just bounces off me now. But when someone brings your son into it, that is when you are entitled to snap. The things they were saying about what they hoped would happen to Brooklyn are too disgusting to repeat. You can't even begin to imagine what goes through the minds of these people.

The songs had only ever been about Brooklyn once before when Leeds United came to Old Trafford. I stuck a finger up at the away end and the Football Association sent Graham Bean, their compliance officer, to come and have a quiet word with me. He said he understood the abuse I was getting but that I needed to control myself. I said I would try but told him it is impossible when your family, and especially your child, are being talked about like that.

There were about eight or nine of them right up close in Eindhoven. They were on the other side of the plastic tunnel down to the dressing room. If that barrier had not been there, I don't know what I might have done. I don't think anyone could have blamed me if I had taken the law into my own hands. They were there in England shirts and tracksuits like any other fans but they had a look of total hate. If anyone could have heard what was said, they would not have criticised me for punching them.

I heard a couple of Sky presenters saying I shouldn't have stuck my finger up, but I would like to see how they would react if someone wished their son dead. I don't think any of the people who criticised me for it in the press were in a position to comment because they've never experienced anything like it. They're keen to get a story and sell papers. Anyway, more people stuck up for me than were against me, which made me feel a bit better about the whole thing.

Kevin Keegan had a word with me about it afterwards. He had to take a fair bit of stick when he was a player, and he told me that there will always be jealous people. He said that I just have to show them that I can keep my head down and enjoy my life because I have so much to look forward to. I'm the one going home to a loving family, a lovely little boy and a wonderful wife so I have to try not to let people like that bother me. He had reacted a few times himself, he said, and that I should learn from mistakes he had made.

I've got a lot of respect for Kevin Keegan but the way he stuck up for me over that incident made me like him even more. There are some managers who would have said, 'It's your mistake. You go and apologise in front of the cameras.' But Alex Ferguson and Kevin Keegan are alike in the way they defend their players to the press. If either of them has an opinion, they'll tell you about it privately afterwards. That's the way it should be.

What the manager said made me even more determined not to let a few idiots spoil the enjoyment of playing for my country. You wouldn't be human if you didn't wonder whether it was all worth it sometimes. But then I think why should I let people like that deprive me of England caps. I want to play for my country as many times as I can and I am not going to walk away because of a few stupid people. That would be damaging myself and I will never let them win. I am prepared to put up with it. I won't let anyone ruin my career.

A story came out in the *Mirror* about what had actually been shouted at me, and how bad the abuse had got. It was all over the front page and I was glad it came out. This wasn't the first time. The abuse had been going on for two years. At least more people now know what I have to put up with sometimes. It wasn't nice to read but maybe it helps others to understand why I react sometimes like I do. I think the other England players were shocked by what they heard and realised that I don't get upset without good reason. I don't want to be treated any differently from any of the other players.

Victoria was at the Portugal game and she got a bit of abuse. She always gets some idiot having a go at her when she comes to games. A story came out that she was travelling separately to the other wives on a private jet because she thought she was too good for them. If she does travel on her own, it is because it saves her getting all that grief. She couldn't come to the Germany match because she was working in the studio but she would have done even after all the problems against Portugal. Victoria loves coming to the matches and I love her being there although sometimes it's better when she's at home and I know she's safe. I'm not always sure how good the security is going to be at a game and I worry about the abuse she gets. She doesn't know a lot about football but she likes to watch me play. She isn't afraid of telling me when I've played badly either.

I think the incident at the end of the Portugal game might have been a turning point. I hope so. I don't normally dare to drive with the roof down in my car but, after the friendly reception in London when I got back from the tournament, I might even start to soon. I am sure I will still get some abuse. I know I am never going to stop that completely but I think more and more people realised at Euro 2000 that I am always trying my best whether it is for club or country.

It lifted me playing against Germany to hear the fans singing my name. It was the first time it has happened at an England game and I guess it was a response to everything that had happened against Portugal. They started it in the warm-up and I felt great. The support of the fans makes a big difference to the players. I want to turn up at Wembley and play for my country knowing everyone is behind me. It inspires me.

The Germany game was a good night although I wouldn't say we played well. Everyone was saying that they were the worst German side of all time and slagging off Lothar Matthaus because he was old. But you can never write off the Germans. You only have to look at their record over the years. They are always tough to beat even if they are not playing at their best. That match felt like a cup final when anything can happen, even if it is a Premier League team against a second division outfit.

There was a lot of hype beforehand about it being 34 years since we had beaten Germany in a major tournament. The players read all about it in the papers so we were really up for it. We knew that if we could get Michael Owen and Alan Shearer on the ball we could beat them. That was the basic plan.

We didn't play well but the plan worked in that we got Alan the ball and he scored. When we won the free kick out on the right, Gary Neville came up to me and said that we should take it short and try to build a move up down the flank because it was quite far out. As usual, I just ignored him, which was just as well. Sometimes you get that feeling when you size up a free kick and you fancy your chances. Obviously I was not aiming for Alan at the back post but I knew that if I put it in that area, we would have a chance. I think Michael got a little flick and it came to Alan. In that position, there is no one else in the country you want to be on the end of it. He has taken a lot of criticism over the years so I was happy for him to score that goal before he retired. He takes it all with a pinch of salt but it must still have been especially nice for him to stick that one in.

We were very happy to have beaten Germany but no one went over the top with the celebrations. We headed back to the hotel in Spa with our confidence high, but we knew we hadn't played that well and would have to improve against the Romanians, even though we only needed a draw to get through to the quarter-finals.

Maybe that was the problem. We knew that a draw was enough and, if there was one mistake, I think we messed up by sitting back too much. After coming back from behind to take a 2-1 lead, we should have been able to kill off the game but we never kept the ball enough and we could hardly complain about losing 3-2.

People always seem to look for individuals to blame, but it would be totally unfair to blame the defeat on Phil Neville. No one was blameless because we never played well even when we took the lead. I was with Phil after the game but there is not a lot you can say. I suppose I understood what he was going through to some extent, after what had happened to me in the World Cup, but I am sure he will not get anything like that abuse. I certainly hope not. One tackle didn't get us knocked out of Euro 2000.

I think I had a good tournament personally although that is not much consolation. I still feel I can do more at international level if I play in the middle. It is frustrating at times being stuck out on the right flank. Playing there for United is easier because you know that the players will find you automatically. With England, you don't have the time together to develop that understanding and I feel that I don't get involved enough.

I tend to move into the middle when I am not getting the ball, and that probably showed in the second two matches at Euro 2000. I want to move to the middle permanently at some stage. I think I will have more influence and do better for England. I felt I did well in the three games and I was involved in some of the goals. Crossing is one of my main strengths, but there is more to my game than that and I want to do more.

Everyone has said their piece about where it went wrong. I don't think the manager or staff could have done any more and I cannot speak highly enough about Kevin Keegan. He did a lot for me on a personal basis. I think he understands my life because he has had to deal with the celebrity situation himself. He is the sort of person I feel I can talk to and he always backed me. It makes a big difference having a manager you can go to for a chat.

It is easy for people to have a go at England players and compare us to Italy and Spain. They have been doing that for as long as I can remember. I think it is harsh because we have had players who have gone there and done well for years. Steve McManaman has won the European Cup with Real Madrid and I am convinced that plenty of the England squad could do well if they went abroad. The thing is that most of them are happy where they are.

I genuinely believe the Premier League is the most exciting in the world. We rely on different strengths from Italy or Spain, but I don't think that makes us any worse as footballers. English teams have done well in Europe over a long period. Liverpool, Nottingham Forest and Aston Villa dominated the European Cup in the 1980s and I think Manchester United have proved that we can hold our own now.

The standard in England has improved in the last five or 10 years. A lot of people put that down to the number of imports but, just as I have learnt things from the foreign players at our club, I am sure they have learnt from us as well. We keep being told that foreign players practise more than us but I think that has changed. I bet at most clubs you will see some players there in the afternoon working on something. The majority at United do.

Maybe we play too many games in this country, which doesn't help. I know we play more league matches than in Italy and there are times when you feel you need a rest. Alex Ferguson left me out a few times in the season and even though I hate not playing, you have to accept that he is right. He can spot without you telling him if you are starting to slow down a bit. He let Peter Schmeichel go to Barbados for a break in the season a couple of years ago and it definitely helped him to be at his best for the rest of the campaign.

But it doesn't depress me looking at how we played at Euro 2000 compared to Italy or France or Holland. It is something to contend with and a challenge that I want to meet with England because I do believe we have the players to succeed. No one can look at our squad and convince me that we cannot mount a serious challenge for future championships with some of the young, talented players coming through, provided that the fans get behind us. The one good thing to come out of the European Championship is that the vast majority of supporters are behind every England player, including those of us who play for Manchester United, because we always give our best.

CHAPTER 7
FAME & FORTUNE

I have a camera up my backside almost 24 hours a day. If I do anything, I have to be prepared for it to be in the newspapers. If I go out and eat five Big Macs I know that will make the news. It can be a hell of a pressure to live with sometimes. I know I will be judged for everything I do. That is why I don't point the finger at other people when they make mistakes, even though it would be very easy for me to do. You should just let everyone get on with their own lives and do what they think is right and hope you will be treated the same way.

I had quite a bit of coverage in the papers before I moved up to Manchester, so I'd already had a little taste of fame. People started talking about me and I slowly got used to it. I liked it back then because if people saw you in the newspapers, they'd start looking out for you on the pitch. I'd always rather read about myself in the football pages than in the gossip columns.

Newspaper coverage is inevitable as a footballer but the madness really started when people found out Victoria and I were seeing each other. It hit the front page and it's been non-stop since then. I was used to being in the papers, but it was completely different from being hounded the way we are now. I've never got used to it. We expect to get a certain amount of coverage and people following us, but it's a bit ridiculous the way it happens everywhere we go, even down to the supermarket. We still find it weird.

You have to watch everything you do. Before we step out of the house we have to make sure we look okay. It's part of every-day life now. Victoria and I stick together through everything and I'm much happier when I'm out with her. It can be a bit uncomfortable at times to be out on my own.

My mates can't believe all the stuff that goes on. They saw it when we were in Brazil and thought it was just ridiculous. The photographers were trying to get pictures of me with other women and it was like that wherever we went, even just walking down the road. Luckily I can control that.

I never go out without being recognised. It's better in places like LA but in Britain and Europe it's impossible to be anonymous. It's frightening. I can't understand the level of interest in every detail of our lives. How can people be so interested in us that it's front-page news if we go shopping, wear something different or get our hair cut? There are so many things happening around the world that should be on the front page instead of us. The newspapers put us there because it sells the papers. In a documentary I saw the other day, there was a girl saying she really hates us but she goes and buys magazines and watches anything we are on because she wants to find out what we're doing and what Victoria's wearing. It's a strange fascination.

Quite often when I'm driving down a motorway, some idiots will spot me and try to drive up close, waving stuff at me or trying to attract my attention. There were always going to be some people who said I should not have got off the speeding charge. I was being tailed bumper to bumper by a photographer. It happens all the time, whether it is journalists or just people who recognise me. I have to cope with all that attention constantly without losing my cool.

The only time I almost lost it was when I came out of the Oxo Tower in London with Victoria. We'd been for a quiet meal but when we left the restaurant, two photographers jumped out of nowhere and started taking pictures. One of them knocked against Victoria and that really annoyed me. It was like an ambush and I have to admit that I almost flipped. The trouble was that there were two of them, so I couldn't win. While I was confronting the one that banged into Victoria, the other was taking pictures. They always get what they want out of you anyway. They can probably sell the photos for more money if they've got you looking annoyed and if you do hit them, they are going to try to sue you. There is nothing you can do.

There is no point in running away from photographers or the press, because they're always going to get you. If you do try to run away from them, they just think you've got something to hide. When we came out of the hospital with Brooklyn, they thought there must be something wrong with him because we didn't want him photographed. That's the sort of mentality you're up against. We still don't like Brooklyn being photographed when we're out and we make sure the media know that. But basically you've got to be a bit lenient with the photographers to get some peace. The trade-off is that we usually let them take photos of the two of us instead. We have to give Brooklyn as normal a life as possible.

I have to accept that there are times when, as part of the Manchester United or England teams and because of my sponsorship deals, I need the press. In a way, we use the press for our own benefit, or for the good of, say, the England team, to try to get the country behind us. There are a certain number of interviews that you've got to do, which I don't really enjoy. Even though I'm still shy, I've got used to making personal appearances for Adidas and Brylcreem, and being with Victoria has also helped me become less shy. I've learnt not to say too much in interviews and I'm far less likely to slip up now than I was.

It would be great to be anonymous again, just to enjoy the simple things, like being able to walk anywhere or stroll into any restaurant. I'm not complaining about my life because I chose to be a footballer and I want to try to be the best in the world. I like the attention on the pitch so I know I have to live with it off the pitch. But it isn't always easy.

We can't go out to a lot of places that we would like to. We'd like nothing better than to wander down to a village pub but it is almost impossible. We might be able to get away with having a drink in the places near my parents' house because they know me there, but any new place is a waste of time. Even if you don't get mobbed, which happens in a lot of places, you still have a constant stream of people asking for autographs. I don't mind signing them but it can be difficult if you are trying to have a quiet night. Your food gets cold by the time you've finished. That is why we go to places like The Ivy in London where they don't allow autograph hunters. It's not to be flash, it's so we know we won't be bothered for one meal.

I have never turned down a reasonable request for an autograph. There might be times when you are in a rush and cannot do one for everyone, but I try to do as many as I can because I know how much it meant to me as a kid to get your heroes to sign something. Bryan Robson gave me his when I was a kid and I can still remember how happy I was. Adidas, Brylcreem and Pepsi might get me to do signings and it can go on for hours sometimes, but it's not the worst part of the job at all.

I was at Crystal Palace once when I was young and I wanted Daley Thompson's autograph but he was busy and I didn't get it. That affected the way I looked at him, and that is why I try to sign them all. Being a dad makes you want to help kids as well. If Brooklyn wants autographs from film stars or whoever, I'll try to help him get them. The only time I will say no to signing is if someone is rude.

The amount of mail I get is amazing and most of it is supportive. I get so much that I pay someone at Old Trafford to go through it all for me and sort out the good from the bad. It keeps her busy because I must get two or three of those big Royal Mail sacks every week, with hundreds and hundreds of letters and parcels. I try to go in once or twice a week and respond to them all. I can spend two or three hours each time just signing replies to letters and reading what has been sent. If I don't do that, I fall behind and I get people coming up asking why I haven't replied.

Obviously I can't read them all in detail or I would spend half my life doing it but the woman who goes through them pulls out some special ones, particularly from young kids, and Tony Stephens, my agent, might bring some to my attention. It won't be the begging letters although I get plenty of those. I had one from someone recently asking me for a Range Rover, which was a bit of a strange request. The person said they were £15,000 in debt and that I could afford to give them my car.

The ones I like to respond to are the genuine ones from people who are ill or have someone in their family who is ill. We pick a few out and I'll give that person a ring at home. You hope it will raise their spirits a bit as they try to deal with their problems. They get a bit surprised when their phone rings and it's someone on the other end saying, 'It's David Beckham here.' I remember doing it just after Euro 2000 when I got a very nice letter from a couple of West Ham fans. They had written after all the abuse I had got during the match against Portugal to say that they were disgusted with the behaviour. They said that even though they were West Ham fans they were right behind me with England. One afternoon I just rang them out of the blue to thank them. It wasn't a long conversation but, if someone has made an effort like that, it is nice to repay it.

The hardest letters to read are the ones from very ill people. It is difficult to help every time, but Victoria and I will try to do what we can. There was one little girl from near Manchester who was terminally ill so we arranged with her mum to go round and see her one day, and I arranged a couple of tickets for a United game. It's just a gesture but you hope it does some good.

I think footballers have a responsibility to help out. We are very lucky to have the jobs we do and you have to try to show that to the supporters and the public. I am not making out I am a saint but it does annoy me sometimes when I read that players don't do enough for charities and so on. I don't do a lot of high-profile stuff or work on one big charity campaign because they would get overshadowed by all the hype. If I did it as part of a big campaign, I would spend half my time dealing with the publicity. That is no good for the people you are trying to help a lot of the time and sometimes parents of sick children don't want themselves all over the papers. I prefer to deal with people directly. Whatever I do, I can't win. If I did make a big show of doing it, some people would say I was only doing it for the publicity.

It is just as well that I have someone going through the post because I get some weird things. The strangest one recently was a black bra and knickers from one female admirer, a big girl as well from the size of them. Victoria just laughs. She has her admirers as well, so we both get our share of bizarre post. Her mum and my mum both keep loads of memorabilia — letters and nice pictures that have been sent to us.

I still get plenty of abusive mail but most of it is kept away from me. I like to see some of it just to see what people are saying. There is so much crap that comes through you wouldn't believe it. It goes straight in the bin so you wonder why people bother. Most of it is predictable stick, but you also get some weird and disgusting messages. You have to ignore it otherwise it would get you worried thinking what sort of people are out there, especially when they know your address. The newspapers printed the name of the town where I live in Cheshire, which is not exactly a big place. All the photographers know it and it is not that hard for people to find, if they are that desperate.

I am satisfied with how I have coped with all the abuse and attention over the past two or three years when you consider how bad it has been sometimes. I haven't gone around punching people or upsetting them by turning down requests to pose for pictures or sign this or that. If you have had to deal with someone trying to snatch your kid, as happened outside Harrods last year, you hope you can cope with anything. That was the worst of all. No one should ever have to worry about the safety of their family like that. We had to get some security in for a while. It was terrifying.

There are more good points to the celebrity lifestyle than bad ones. I would be lying if I said that I don't get a buzz sometimes from being centre stage, although that's mostly on the pitch. That is where it really matters to me. The down side is that you can feel trapped sometimes. We feel we have to lock the door and close the curtains before we can get any privacy at all. We can't even throw photographers off the scent because they know the registrations of our cars, where we live, our parents' addresses and where we like to go out. Some people say we are like the royal family. There is some similarity in the sort of media pressure we are all put under, but I don't like to make comparisons. I can stop being a footballer but they will always be royals and I don't think you can know what that is like unless you are part of it.

I think we've had so much attention that we'd miss it if it suddenly went away. If Victoria and I had to make a choice between retiring from our work and leaving the limelight, or carrying on doing our own thing and putting up with the loss of privacy, there would be no contest. Neither of us has a choice because we would hate not to be doing the work we are doing, even if that means we are under constant scrutiny. So we'd rather the way it is than any other right now.

The way to deal with it all in the future might be through having my own web site. I have been talking to people about it, and it's something that I want to get involved in. Ole Gunnar Solskjaer at United has his own web site and uses it to tell fans what's going on in his life. Other players have web sites too and use them to put the record straight if there are rumours or stories floating around. It would be a good chance for me to communicate directly with the fans and it might take some of the pressure off me with the press always trying to find out about my life.

I don't think that I have changed fundamentally with all the attention. People say that I am doing things like the tattoos just for show, but I would have had them even if I wasn't a footballer and I was working in a garage. Why should I hide them, particularly when people will find out about them anyway? I do them for myself. If other people want to judge, it is up to them.

I know Alex Ferguson said that I've lost my sense of fun in recent years but I don't agree. I think the reason he says that is because I've lost that way of being in front of people. I express it more when I'm with friends and family, in private. I still have a lot of fun but not too much when people are watching. People may look at me and say I'm miserable all the time, but I'm not. So many things have happened in my life and career that sometimes I'm a bit bitter because of all the crap I have to put up with. It's just made me a little more guarded. The whole experience after Argentina inevitably affected how I go about my life and some of my relationships with people, but basically I am the same person. I'm sure everyone who knows me well would agree with that.

I'm determined not to let the bad bits spoil my life. Victoria and I are both in a very fortunate position. We have jobs we love and which are well paid. We are well aware of that and never want to take it for granted. Footballers earn good money but I don't just sit around and think 'I'm loaded'. I can understand that people think footballers have a great life but I like to feel that I work for my money. There is an obsession with players' wages in the press and among the public but it is not like that with the players. At least, it isn't among the United lads.

A few papers were trying to stir it up when Roy Keane got his new contract which was reported as being worth around £50,000 a week. They said I was sulking and moping around because I was on half that. Whatever a player can get out of the club, good luck to him. Roy is worth whatever he is on. He's a world-class player. He got a bit of the usual stick about buying the next round and all the jokes you would expect, but I am not the type to get annoyed by what someone else is earning. I am not a jealous person. Provided I am happy, I just get on with my own job and let everyone else take care of their own life. More money doesn't automatically make you happier anyway. If there is jealousy in a team, it will create problems straightaway and I don't see any signs of people falling out with each other at Old Trafford.

Like any job, if you work hard and do your job properly you get the going rate. You can just as easily ask whether film stars should earn £10 million for one movie as talk about whether footballers deserve it. I just consider myself lucky that my job is well paid because even if it wasn't I would still be doing it.

Footballers earn peanuts compared to the United States where you have basketball and baseball players on more than double what the best paid footballers here can get. But I am sure that I will never decide my future on where I can earn the most money. Some people need to chase money but that has never been the way I have worked. I have some commercial deals and it is great to be able to go out and buy nice things, but I could do a lot more work away from football if I was obsessed with earning more. Money is not my main motivation.

I can understand why people might get jealous of Victoria and me if they are reading that we are worth £30 million, but we have got nothing like that. They also read that I have spent £2,000 on a pair of jeans and all sorts of ridiculous stories. It would get up my nose too if I read that in a paper. I admit I have spent a lot of money on individual items in the past. I think the most must be £85,000 on a Porsche but I am a lot more careful with my money now that I am a family man. I never used to worry about it but now I like to know where I stand and I am always aware of what is in my account. I'm probably still not as careful with money as I should be and Victoria's a lot more sensible with money than I am. She watches her money all the time and that's probably the right way to be. We have accountants to deal with investments and so on but we are not making any special plans to use our money on long-term projects apart from our house. We like to enjoy ourselves at the moment.

I never went without when I was a child, so money has never been that important to me anyway. My parents always gave me what I wanted and needed, without spoiling me. I wasn't one of those horrible children who had everything. Believe me, I always asked for more, but most of the time I didn't get it. If you're brought up that way, it sets you on the right path in life. It's important to be told no sometimes.

I am trying to apply that to Brooklyn but I just love buying things for him. I buy him clothes and toys and the trucks that he likes. I also love buying clothes for Victoria. I like surprising her and I'd rather give a gift than receive one.

Having said that, I do buy a lot of clothes for myself, I have a real passion for clothes and I have always taken a lot of care with my appearance. Even when we used to play for our Sunday league team, our manager made us wear a shirt and tie for cup matches, which meant that we always looked smarter than the other team. Maybe that's where I got it from.

Some of the things I used to wear a few years ago were horrendous and when I look back, I think, what was I doing. I bought a shirt once. It was white with big red letters on the back. I can't remember what it said but it was the worst item of clothing I've ever bought. I still regret it now. It was even worse than the shell suit I had when I was younger!

I have to wear a suit and shirt for the games and I'm into William Hunt suits at the moment, but apart from that I prefer dressing down. I usually wear tracksuits, combats and jeans. I get dressed up when Victoria and I go out, which is something we've always enjoyed. Victoria is into clothes as well and has really good taste. The way Victoria dressed and the way she came across on the telly attracted me to her in the first place, especially the short skirts and her legs. The clothes she wore and her appearance were always unbelievable and still are.

Victoria and I love shopping for our outfits on a Saturday, then getting ready later, going out and having a great night. Sometimes we go out in the same gear on purpose, but other times we do it without knowing what the other one is going to wear. We just end up in similar clothes. But then, we sometimes say exactly the same thing at exactly the same time, too. I think you have that connection when you're really close to someone. It's always been like that with us, ever since we met.

Victoria has never told me what to wear. Obviously, she buys things for me, but I bought the infamous sarong when I was out with Mel B's ex-husband, Jimmy, in Paris. In fact, I liked it so much, I bought several in different colours and Jimmy bought a couple as well. Jimmy was great to go shopping with because he knew where all the good shops were and he was one of the coolest male dressers I've ever met. So buying the sarong had nothing to do with Victoria. There were probably loads of people out there thinking, what's a man doing in a sarong. What's going through his head? She's wearing the trousers and she's got him wearing a skirt. But some people with broader minds must have thought, well, he looks good in it, so what's the problem? Unfortunately, there aren't enough open-minded people thinking that way.

I knew it was going to cause some sort of a stir. There was always going to be a certain amount of media interest in it. Still, I bought it because I liked it. I've worn it again even though I was slaughtered the first time I was seen in it.

Because I'm a footballer, people expect me to wear the same sort of clothes as other footballers and go out and get drunk and be a man, when in fact a lot of things have changed in society. I don't think we should be sheep and follow anyone else. We're individuals and should be prepared to show that in our behaviour. Clothes are just one way of expressing your individuality, but it's an important one for me. I also think of dressing as a way of being artistic and art is something I'm quite into. I probably would have gone to art school if I hadn't been a footballer. I've always felt the same way. I remember when I was about seven, I was asked to be a pageboy. I had to chose from a couple of outfits when Mum took me shopping. The one I wanted had white socks up to my knees, velvet maroon knickerbockers, white ballet shoes, a frilly Spanish shirt and a matching maroon waistcoat. Mum said, 'Do you realise that people are probably going to laugh at you and think you look stupid?' But I was comfortable in it and felt good, so it didn't bother me what other people might think. I liked it so much that I wore it round the house as well.

I watch fashion programmes sometimes and look through magazines but I'm not that influenced by them. If I see something I like, I get it whether or not it's in fashion. I've got a few items from expensive shops but I don't go in there and spend thousands of pounds, and I never buy things for the sake of it or do 'all sizes, all colours'. I've got a bigger wardrobe than Victoria and I've got more clothes than she has, although I'm quite neat and I know where everything is in there. My dressing room is always tidy and Victoria hates it for that. If anyone ever asks my mum whether I was tidy as a kid, she says, 'He even used to fold up his dirty washing before he gave it to me!' Victoria's dressing room is very untidy. When I have a throw out, I put the stuff I don't wear in bags and they either go to charity shops or to my friends.

I'm very clean and tidy generally and I love to cook. I think that's the way it should be nowadays. I don't agree with having a housewife who does all the running around and domestic stuff for you. I don't see much difference between men and women in that way. My dad's not like that at all. He's much more traditional than I am. He loves my mum, but he's never been affectionate to her in front of my sisters and me and he only cooks once in a blue moon.

When I lived at home, I used to cook breakfast for my mum in the morning now and then and occasionally I'd cook dinner too. I was only young but I really enjoyed it. I'd cook simple things like gammon and chips. These days I can cook most things but I don't do complicated stuff very often. I prefer to cook off the cuff so I never use a recipe. I don't like things that are too spicy but generally I'll try anything. Victoria is a good cook. If we've got friends coming round, she'll often make a lasagne or something. We entertain people at home quite a lot.

Basically, I'm not scared of my feminine side and I think quite a lot of the things I do come from that side of my character. People have pointed that out as if it's a criticism, but it doesn't bother me. I think it's good for men to be in touch with their feminine side. I suppose I get the male side out by playing football. Maybe that's the modern equivalent of hunting for me, that and my love of cars.

I'm lost without a car and I absolutely adore driving, which Victoria finds weird. I feel relaxed when I'm behind the wheel but I hate being a passenger. That makes me feel totally out of control. I like to be in charge and know which way I'm going or I'm not comfortable in a car. If I'm on my own and I can't sleep, I'll go out for an hour's drive at two o'clock in the morning. Sometimes it's hard to unwind because I can't stop thinking about things. I worry about what's going on in my life and whether Victoria and Brooklyn are okay, particularly when they're not with me.

My favourite toy at playschool was a police car and my mum and dad have pictures of me standing by sports cars all through my childhood. My first car was an Escort but I always wanted a Porsche. It was brilliant when I was able to buy one with my first pay cheque from Adidas. I got fed up with it, though, because it sat in the driveway for ages and I never drove it. I swapped it for a TVR because I got a good deal on the Porsche from the TVR garage. The papers say I've got eight cars, but it's not true. I've actually got a Ferrari, a TVR and a big Jeep. The Ferrari was a present from Victoria and it's incredible. I absolutely adore it and I'd never want to sell it. It's the best present Victoria has given me, apart from Brooklyn, and the best car I've ever driven. The Jeep is for family trips. I might get another car if a really nice new one came out, something like a convertible Ferrari, but I'm not in any hurry for one.

Obviously, Victoria and I have no money troubles and can afford most luxuries, which neither of us take for granted. But apart from that, we live fairly quiet, normal lives and enjoy doing the same sorts of things other couples do. A lot of the time when we are together at home, we stay in and watch television or a film. We both love watching films. My favourite actor is Hugh Grant, and Julia Roberts and Sandra Bullock are my favourite actresses. Another thing we both enjoy is going to art galleries when we get a chance. We've collected quite a few pieces. Most of it is modern art but basically we will buy anything if we both like it.

I've never been one to go out and drink 15 pints, or to stagger out of a nightclub and stop for a curry on the way home. I'll have a drink for a special occasion. If I do drink, I am more of a wine and champagne man because I never get a headache with champagne. People will have a go now, saying I am big-time but it is just what I like to drink and what I find best for me. At home I drink wine. I'm not an expert, but we have a small collection of wines that we've bought or been given as presents. A red wine from Tuscany is my favourite. When I go out with Victoria and it's just the two of us, we sometimes get a bit drunk on wine and have a laugh. The night we won the European Cup, Victoria flew in to celebrate and the whole team was all over the place. We were allowed to let go because it was our last game of the season.

About once a month, all the players and the management go out together for the day and I'll have a drink then. The captain organises it, depending on the games we've got and when we've got them. Days out like that help to maintain team spirit and create a good atmosphere among the players. It means that we're not just spending all our time in football, we're going out and having a laugh outside it as well. I think most football teams do it. After training, we go home for a couple of hours and meet up around 2 p.m. when we'll go to a quiet pub for lunch and a few drinks. Most of the time, we just take the mickey out of each other and have a laugh. We don't talk about football much, but if something has happened in a game or someone's made a mistake, they get the mickey taken. When I had my hair cut, it was my turn. There are a few players in the team with skinheads and the others keep messing our names up. I've had quite a bit of stick over other things as well. Occasionally, I don't go, if Victoria is in Manchester and I haven't seen her in a while.

Our social life is mostly pretty low key, but then it has to be because of my job. I have to be fairly disciplined particularly during the season, which means that Victoria and I have to be selective about what parties we go to. We always have been because we don't want to be known as a couple that goes to the opening of an envelope. I think most professional football teams and the individual players are very strict about what they get up to the night before a game or even for the few nights before a game. If I've got a game on Wednesday and Saturday, I'll have a very quiet week. For the last few months of last season, we had a game Saturday and Wednesday most weeks, so it was pretty tough. The team didn't have the chance to go out for the day in a long time.

I have never had a strict routine as such. The night before a game I'm in bed by 11. If we are playing at home, I get up pretty much when I wake up, at about 10. I'll have a light breakfast, just some cereal, but I'm not a big eater in the mornings anyway. I'm quite lucky in that I could eat pretty much what I like and still keep my fitness. A lot of players have to be very careful about their diet. Steak and chips is my favourite, but I don't indulge myself all the time or I might end up putting on weight. At the club, we all sit down to lunch before the match. I don't eat the poached and scrambled eggs that a lot of the players like. I usually have tomato soup and the chef will do me some sweet and sour pork with rice.

I'm not the most punctual when it comes to getting to Old Trafford. Gary and Phil Neville are always there right on time. They're never late for anything but I am often rushing in five or 10 minutes late because I have been playing with Brooklyn at home. I'm not the superstitious type so I don't tie one lace before the other or put on my right sock before my left deliberately. Paul Ince would always keep his shirt off until he was running out of the tunnel. Now Andy Cole and Dwight Yorke hang around until the end because they like to be last out on the pitch. At least now I've had my hair cut off, I don't have to do the hair routine before I play. I used to get quite a bit of stick for that from the other players because while everyone else was putting on their boots and shin pads, I'd be sat in the corner putting gel in my hair.

However you do it, the important thing is to be physically and mentally prepared and all of the team including me are very focused in that way. Preparation for matches is part of your life all the time.

We did go clubbing quite a bit during the summer while I was off, which was good because we don't often get the chance to go to clubs together. While we were in the South of France we had a memorable night out with Janet Street-Porter and Patrick Cox. We all went to a gay club and Victoria told me I had five minutes to see if the men there could turn me gay. While she danced on the stage, all these men gathered on the dance floor and danced in front of me. It doesn't bother me at all to have gay men fancying me. Being around the Spice Girls and the dancers on their tours has got me used to the idea. We've been to quite a few gay bars and it's always great fun. In London, we might go to Browns and a few other places, often with my friend Dave Gardiner and Victoria's sister Louise.

You get a lot of hangers-on and I can spot them from miles away, just by their looks and the way they are behaving. I never get involved with them. I suppose that does mean that we have to be a bit careful about who we spend time with. Even people who are nice and not hangers-on at all can be a bit uncomfortable around Victoria and me. This celebrity thing can make it hard for people to be themselves. I remember one time I was at Victoria's parents' house. Jackie had advertised an old wardrobe for sale and a couple came round to see it. Then Victoria and I walked in and it was quite funny seeing their faces as they tried to work out if it was really us or not. When Victoria walked downstairs, they were probably thinking, no, it can't be. But when I came down with Brooklyn in my arms, they looked at us, looked at each other, looked back at us and looked at each other again. Then we walked out. You could see them thinking, maybe we just dreamt that.

We normally spend time with our close friends and families. My best friends are Dave Gardiner and Gary Neville. I talk to Gary about personal things. He's always there to give me advice and he's always there if I'm worried about something. That's why we're such good friends. When I had problems with Alex Ferguson, Gary was the one I spoke to about it all. He's like the brother I never had.

I met him when I first moved to Manchester when I was 16. We've always been good friends, but I think we've developed a stronger relationship over the past few years because we've spent so much time together and grown up together. It's almost like a marriage we're so close. We work together and socialise together and we confide in each other about everything. He's the only person apart from Victoria that I could say absolutely anything to.

CHAPTER 8
CAPTAIN OF ENGLAND

Some people seem to think that 2000-2001 was an average season for me but I think that is just a sign of how far I have already come. I finished the season as captain of an England team that is on a roll under the new manager and Manchester United won the championship with weeks to spare — not bad for a mediocre year. As for my private life, that could not be better and I left for my summer holidays with Victoria and Brooklyn feeling as contented as at any time in my life.

The England captaincy was obviously the biggest thing to happen to me and it still amazes me every time I look back and think how I was treated just a few years ago. If someone had said in 1998 after my sending-off in the World Cup that I would be leading my country out within three years, I would have laughed in their face.

The World Cup qualifying match we lost against Germany in October was a turning point in England's fortunes. Kevin Keegan resigned and Tony Adams retired not long after and there was a lot of talk about a new era with young players. We needed to make some changes but I will never say a bad word about Kevin. When he resigned in the dressing room after the Germany game it was a massive shock, coming totally out of the blue. I don't think even the people closest to him knew what he was going to do but I think the way the fans were after the game helped him to make his decision. It still took courage to come out and say that he had done his bit but had to step down.

I rang him about two months after he resigned just to say hello and to see how he was. I will always respect him for what he did for me. He had been in a similar position to me, dealing with the pressures of celebrity, and he went out of his way to help me through those problems. I really appreciated all his help and I think that he was glad for the call.

I was delighted when I heard that he had taken the job at Manchester City. Some people may have got on his back after the England situation but I never doubted that he would have the confidence to return, and it is a sign of his self-belief that he was willing to take on a big job like City. I hope he can get them back into the Premiership — a derby match with him in the opposite dug-out would be great.

After Kevin left the England job, Peter Taylor made me captain against Italy. I was chuffed when Sven-Goran Eriksson told me I could keep the armband. We did not have any special meeting or anything. He just told me in the team hotel before the match against Spain that it had been mine before he came and I deserved to keep it. I like to think that I have risen to the challenge.

During my career, I have always liked to have new ambitions and goals. Leading my country is something that has helped me to progress as a person and player. A lot was said when I first took the job about whether I was a natural leader or not. Maybe I'm not but I have done the job in the way that I think is best and, so far, the players and manager seem happy with how I go about it.

Apart from the responsibilities on the pitch, there are issues away from the games when I have to act as the link between the players and the manager. It might just be little things. At our training camp in La Manga, for instance, some of the players were not sure whether they were allowed to play golf in their free time and came to me to find out the rules. Some people might find that a pain but I have enjoyed the responsibility. I know how important it is to have good bonding between everyone in the camp and I just try to make sure everyone is at ease.

The job of captain is very easy under Sven anyway because of the coolness and calmness that he has brought to the team. I think we have struck up a very good relationship and I enjoy talking to him about the game. I had to pop into the FA headquarters in May to sort out some bits and pieces and he was in his office so we had a good chat about how the team was progressing.

Sven will say just what he needs to say and no more. People have the same respect for him that they have for Alex Ferguson at United because they can instantly tell that he knows what he is doing and that he is the man in charge. Five consecutive victories should have proved to everyone that his methods work.

We started well in the friendly against Spain and I played my best game for England against Finland at Anfield in March. I even got to hear my name sung out by the Kop. Maybe being captain helped but I also hope that supporters — even Liverpool ones — realise that I give everything for my country. I was very happy with my performance that day, especially the goal.

The weird thing was that when I went back to Liverpool with Manchester United the next week, the abuse from the terraces was worse than ever. People think we are making a big deal out of it if Victoria doesn't go to a game, but the stick that day proved why. I had heard most of it before, but the amount was unbelievable. I have resigned myself to the fact that it will never end. All that matters is that I can deal with it and I think I have done a good job of keeping my cool. It would be nice to be like Gazza who was loved by all England fans whatever club he played for and when I am in an England shirt, I hope that can still happen.

People have said that Gary Neville, Paul Scholes and I have improved under Sven. It is also part of the growing-up process. We realised that we weren't the youngsters in the squad any more. When it was the young ones against the old ones, we were on the wrong side. We are the experienced ones now and it is up to us to show the way. Playing for United helps because we are used to the big occasions. The older players should always help. I remember when I first came in and Alan Shearer and Paul Ince talked to me. I was so grateful for that.

I hope that my performances against Mexico and Greece at the end of the season showed people that it does not matter what haircut you have as long as you are doing your best for the team and behaving properly on the pitch. So much was said about my Mohican, most of it rubbish, but I can say that one person who does not care about it is the England coach. He is more concerned about football than trivial matters and, despite what people have said, Alex Ferguson is the same.

If anyone thinks the haircut was inspired by Robert de Niro in *Taxi Driver* they should think again. I have never even seen the film. The plain truth is that I was bored with the shaven look and fancied trying something different. I thought the Mohican might be quite fun and was going to do it during the summer holidays. As it happened, I had the chance to do it earlier and, even if some people didn't like it, I can't believe they thought it made me unfit to captain my country.

Most people found it quite funny and I loved it when I heard there was an 88-year-old woman who had decided to have one as well. My team-mates certainly had a good joke about it. They kept singing the theme tune to the *A-Team* when I came into the dressing room and I was nicknamed BA Baracas for a while. Generally, I don't plan things, they just happen on the day. A haircut is only a haircut after all.

I prefer to talk about England's performances which were some of the best I have been involved in, not just from a personal point of view but also as a team. I think each of the World Cup qualifiers against Finland, Albania and Greece showed an improvement from one to the next, finishing with the high of the 2-0 victory in Athens. Of course, we know we have to get better still, but what matters is that we are eager to learn.

Probably the best quality we have learnt under our new coach is to be patient and stick to our good habits even when we are going through a bad spell. Bad spells are always going to happen at international level when the competition is so intense. I know that, in the past, sometimes we have panicked at those times and that is when you start lumping it forward just to clear your own lines.

If there is one thing that Sven has stressed it is that we must not just be hitting balls over the top of the opposition defence and then trying to get it back. There are times, especially when you have players as fast as Michael Owen, when the direct ball can work, but most of the play has to be crisp passes with a compact team. We know we have enough good players to ensure that the goals will come if we are patient and keep playing to our strengths.

We know things are not always going to be smooth but the age of this side tells me that we can do something special over the next few years. We know we have the players and the manager to start making a real impact. I have been lucky to win so much with United and it is my dream to be successful with England. There have been so many doubters about the England side since I was first picked for the squad and it is time that we started making the whole country proud. I know that we are only starting on a long path but I hope everyone can see that we are heading in the right direction.

There are plenty of players coming in and making a huge impression. I have been struck by the talents of Steven Gerrard now that I have had a chance to play alongside him a few times. England have needed someone like him in central midfield for a while, a rock alongside Scholesy. He can pass and shoot, and everyone knows that he can tackle as strongly as anyone. I remember about three minutes into our victory over Mexico at Pride Park when I was fouled and he came flying in with a real hard but fair challenge. It didn't matter that he plays for Liverpool and I play for Manchester United. We were united for England and willing to stick up for each other. That is how good the team spirit is now. At United, Roy Keane takes that role but I would compare Steve more with Patrick Vieira who is another great midfield player whom I respect so much. Steve is gangly like Patrick and gets to balls with those long legs when you think he has no chance. He has not only added his own strengths but helped to bring out the best of the rest of us alongside him.

I would say the overall team play was at its best against Greece and my only complaint that night was the barrage of missiles from the terraces. We had all been warned about it before kick-off but the amount still came as a surprise with lighters, coins, bottles and all sorts raining down. I ended up with a couple of marks on my back where I was hit by coins and, if people thought a couple of my corners were not up to my usual standard, I can only hope that they will understand why I was rushing them.

Luckily, the England fans were throwing only compliments. It was another great reception at the end of the game, which sent me off on my summer holidays in the best possible mood. You can't imagine how happy I was to be going off with Victoria and Brooklyn on the back of those victories, but I felt just the same as the manager when he said that he would miss being with the squad.

By the time we played Mexico and Greece, Steve McClaren had dropped out of the England camp but I think we showed that you have to be able to move on from those disruptions, even if Steve is a great coach. We have always said at United that the club is bigger than anyone and I am sure we will be able to move on too, now that Steve has gone to be manager of Middlesbrough. The real test will come when Alex Ferguson leaves Old Trafford at the end of this season. There has already been plenty of speculation about his position and successors, but the players will have to get on with the job of winning trophies and not get distracted. Everyone will want to send the manager off on a high, especially with the European Cup final at Hampden Park in May, but we can't try any harder than we already do to win trophies.

Everyone will miss having him in charge, me included, because he is a legend as a manager. A lot has been said about our relationship over the years but he has always wanted what is best for my career and I owe him a lot. Determination comes from inside each player but it was the manager who brought us together and made us into a real team. The way he wants to win everything, from the team quizzes to European Cups, has rubbed off on us down the years.

It will be a weird year, an emotional year, for the club because the manager has been a father figure to a lot of the young players coming through and it would be great if he could finish his last game lifting the European Cup. The biggest disappointment of last season for me was not playing against Bayern Munich when we went out in the quarter-final second leg. I had been suspended for a tackle on Stefan Effenberg. Players wind each other up and a few little things went on on the pitch. Effenberg is a good player and we were just having a little battle. I was gutted to pick up a yellow card because it meant I was helpless in front of the television when the rest of the lads were trying their best in Munich.

I don't know if I could have made a difference to the result, but I do know that I was in good enough form to give it a real go. A lot has been said, most of it rubbish, about me being found out by some teams but I felt a better player at the end of last season than I did at the start. I won't deny that I had a dip in form - who doesn't? - but it was always going to be hard to maintain the early burst when I was scoring more goals than I had at any time in my career. I started getting tired towards the end and suffered a bout of flu but I thought I was back at my best after a rest. Three goals in four England games should have showed that.

If it was tougher in the European games, I think it might have been because I was double-teamed a bit more with two or three players closing me down. As a player you have to get used to that and also realise that you can sacrifice yourself for the good of the team. If I can drag their defenders around, it will leave space behind the left-back for others to exploit.

I hope that I am still progressing as a player and learning new ways of helping the team. I have worked on cutting infield more and I also think I have got more control of my temperament, although I would never want to get rid of the hunger that drives me on. I picked up less than a handful of yellow cards and no red ones and it was just unfortunate that when I was suspended, it was for a European Cup quarter-final. Playing for England, I am glad that I managed to get on with my game even when I was being struck by missiles in Greece.

It can't have been that bad a season when I think that we won the championship and, from a personal point of view, I finished just two votes behind Teddy Sheringham for the journalists' Footballer of the Year. At United, we have set such high standards that every year we don't win the European Cup now is regarded as a failure. We will have to win it again if we want to be up among clubs such as Real Madrid, AC Milan and Juventus who have got to finals time after time.

We didn't step our game up enough from the Premiership to the Champions League last season but you could be sure that the manager would not allow things to go stale. Even before the end of the season he had broken the British transfer record to buy Ruud van Nistelrooy for £19 million from PSV Eindhoven, and that must scare our rivals because we already had four great strikers on the books.

I started talks about a new contract at United on the day before the FA Cup final and, despite what some of the papers have said, those discussions are not all about money. In fact, money was not even mentioned then. I have always loved playing for United and what matters to me is that I am at a club where I am happy and can be successful and, so far in my career, Old Trafford has provided everything I could want.

CHAPTER 9
THE FUTURE

I know there is a lot of interest in my life and Victoria's and I hope this book gives people an insight into how we live. It is easy for people to read the newspapers and get the wrong idea that we are going from one flash night out to the next. We like a good time but we are both very committed to our families and to being the best at our jobs.

It is not all the glamorous showbiz lifestyle that everyone assumes. When Victoria performed solo at the Party in the Park in London last summer, that was a massive day for her but it was also work. People see pictures of us hanging around backstage with Craig David, Jon Bon Jovi and Prince Charles and think that is what we do all the time. Although we stayed there for a few drinks after she had performed, we went out that night with Victoria's family because it was her brother's birthday the next day. I've never met anyone as committed to their job or as determined to do their best all the time as Victoria.

We do have some friends in showbiz. Elton John was performing at that concert in Hyde Park, and he and his partner David Furniss are good friends. We go out with them from time to time. Elton's brilliant and so down to earth. He's also very funny and we have a great time with him and David. They've helped us out a lot in the past. For instance, when a story breaks and we're getting hassle from the press, they'll be the first ones to phone and ask if we need to get away for a week and they'll invite us to their place in the South of France. As well as being good friends, they're very supportive of what we do. Elton's been there, done it and got the T-shirt, so he's a good person to listen to in a crisis.

When we're out, well-known people may come up and say hello or introduce themselves if we've not met them, which is nice. I think that, out of all of them, one person I enjoyed meeting was Boris Becker, who was on the same table as us at Elton's Barbie evening. I was pleased to meet him because he's a legend. He was great to talk to and it was a real experience to spend some time with him, even though he's a Bayern Munich fan, which didn't go down very well!

We want Brooklyn to live as normal a family life as possible and we try to protect him from being in the newspapers. We would love to be able to take him to the park just like any kid, but we know there will be photographers there and it would be impossible. It makes me sad to think that although Brooklyn is a very lucky boy in a lot of ways, he maybe won't have the freedom and privacy that other children have.

The press interest is always going to be tough. It is very hard to stop the rumours building up all the time, like the one about me moving to a London club just because we bought a house in Hertfordshire. It annoys me because I know lots of the other players have second homes in London or foreign countries, but no one goes on about when they are leaving. We will live near London eventually because that is where our families come from and the new house is perfect for a five-a-side pitch for me and Brooklyn. But at the moment, I play for Manchester United and I live in Manchester and that should be the end of it, although I know it won't be.

People say I should be used to it by now but it annoys me because of what the United fans might believe. I don't want them thinking I am not committed to the club or that I am risking my fitness by driving up and down the M6 every day. I want them to know that I am as dedicated to United now as I was when I first dreamt of playing for the first team as a kid. I wouldn't be able to run if I did as much commuting as some people have said, but it is very hard to stop people believing what they hear.

My contract at United runs out in 2003, the year after Alex Ferguson's does. I don't see any reason why I should not be at Old Trafford until at least then. You never know what the club wants to do and it is a lot more complicated now that players are free agents when their contracts run out. Clubs sometimes sell their best players for financial reasons.

It would be very, very tough to play for another English club at the moment, although you never know what's going to happen in the future. I know I would find it very hard to go to Old Trafford as an opponent. My dad will support me in anything I do but he would find it hard to cheer another team against United, even if I was playing for them. I haven't ruled out going abroad at some stage to prove myself as a top player on the Continent. I think I have done that already with United and England.

Sometimes I wonder if winning the European Cup with United in the Nou Camp was as good as it can ever get, especially the way we won it in the last minute. Winning the World Cup final with England is probably the only way I could equal that. But I've still got the hunger to try to beat that achievement. I am playing for a great club alongside my mates and for people who have supported and helped me for most of my life. There is a unique atmosphere at Old Trafford that you might never find again for the rest of your career. No one knows if it will change when the manager steps down in 2002 so you have got to make the most of it while you can. In football, you can never say that something is forever.

I haven't captained a United team since the Milk Cup in Ireland when I was 16, but I think every footballer wants to be captain. It is a testament to how you are playing, and other players listen to you more. Some people shout and holler in the dressing room but that is not my style. Maybe that wouldn't make me a natural choice but I think I could do the job well. You don't want to shout just for effect. The armband won't be available for years now that Roy Keane has signed a long-term contract at United. Roy has done a great job as skipper. People questioned the choice when the manager gave him the armband but he is a real leader of the team and has proved that time and again.

All I know is that I will keep working hard to be the best, just like Victoria does in her singing career. That is one of the reasons we fell for each other — because we are both determined to get better and better. You need to have your goals for every day and every week. My main ambition is to keep on doing what I'm doing and enjoying myself.

After I've stopped playing, I think I'll have a year off, or perhaps even longer, doing whatever Victoria's doing, going on holiday and doing the things I haven't been able to do all these years. I even want to travel to the moon one day, if that's possible by the time I retire from football. The thought of it terrifies Victoria but I'd love to do it. I want to go skiing the day after I stop playing football. I can't do it now because of the insurance. If I broke my leg on the ski slopes and couldn't play again, I wouldn't be insured. Water sports are out of the question at the moment as well.

I like horses too, and may take up riding. The first time I rode a horse was in Ireland with Victoria. She was sitting up there, very proudly, just how you'd imagine, with the right hat and coat, looking very proper and elegant. It was her suggestion that I tried it. 'Let's go horse riding,' she said. 'I've done it for the last few days and the coach says I'm absolutely excellent. I'll gallop along ahead and you can stay behind us and learn.' So I jumped on a horse and started galloping straightaway. It was fantastic. When it was all over and we got off the horses, Victoria said, 'Surely you've done that before?' She couldn't believe it was my first time, so maybe I'm a natural. People say to me now that I'll have problems with my knees in years to come because of the way I kick the ball, but I haven't had a serious injury so far, touch wood. I feel very fit and really well.

People often ask me where I see myself in 10 years' time. I don't really have any idea of what I'll be doing. I have enough money not to have to work again but I will need to do something when I retire from football. It will be nice to relax for a while and to get away from it all, but there will have to be something to replace the buzz. Eric Cantona gets his from acting. I'm not sure I am cut out for that but I will need to find something. I get very restless with nothing to do. I will want to feel I am doing a proper job for a proper wage.

I just hope I'll be as happy as I am now. I'd like us to have three or four more babies in the next five or six years, which should keep me busy well into my retirement from football. There will be plenty of room for any additions to the Beckham family because we are getting near to finishing our house in the south. We have deliberately taken our time with it because as long as I am playing for United, I will spend most of the week in the north anyway. There are parts of my life that I have found hard to deal with over the last couple of years but I am wiser for it all and the difficulties have made me appreciate everything that is good in my life. I am healthy and I have a lovely family and a great life. I wouldn't want to change anything in the past. As for the future, as long I stay healthy and my family stays healthy, that's all that bothers me. Health and happiness — that's it.

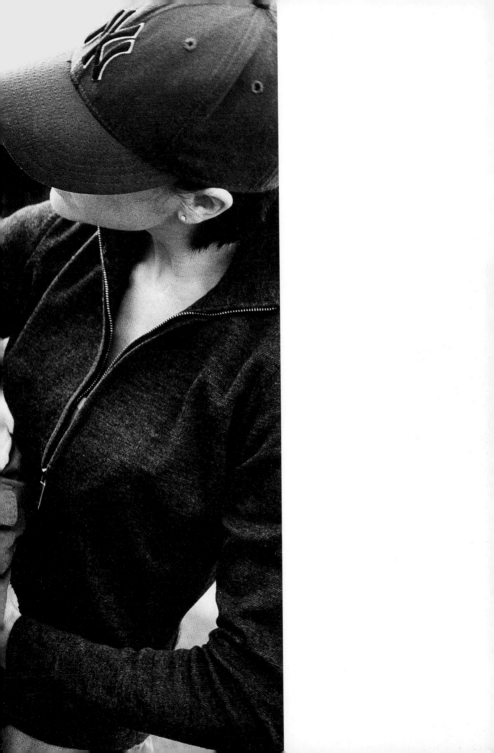

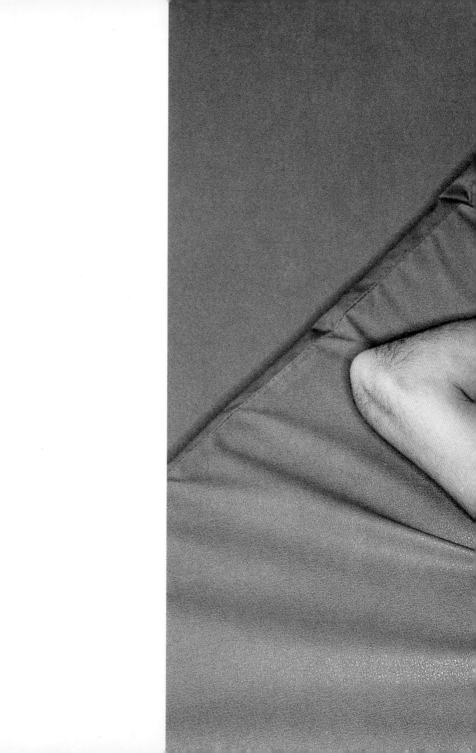

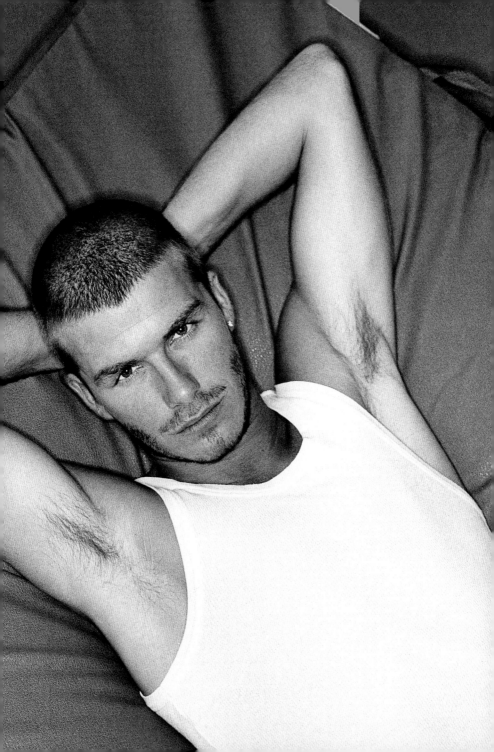

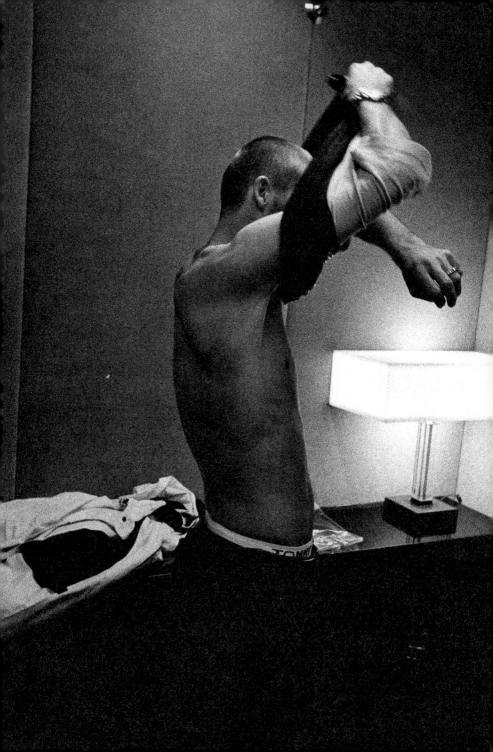

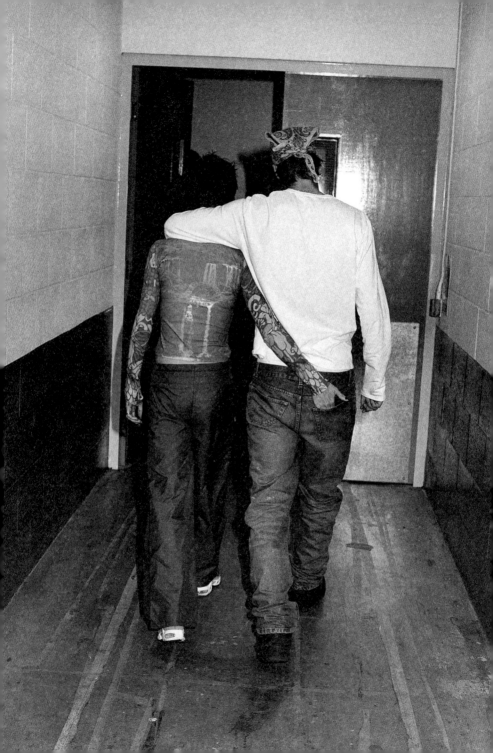

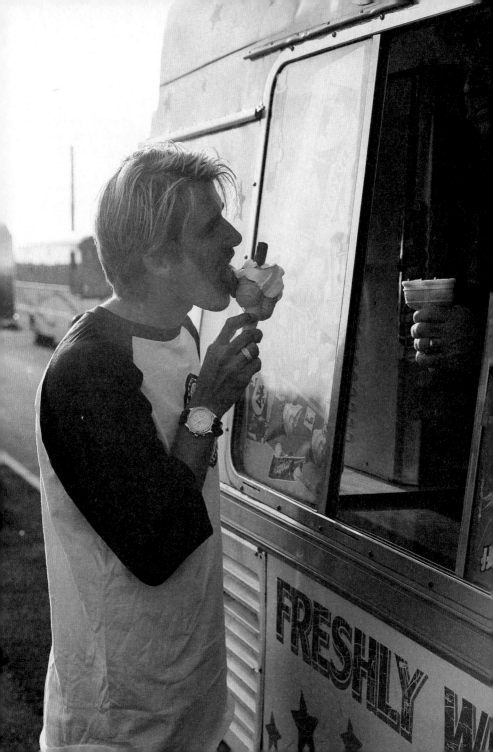

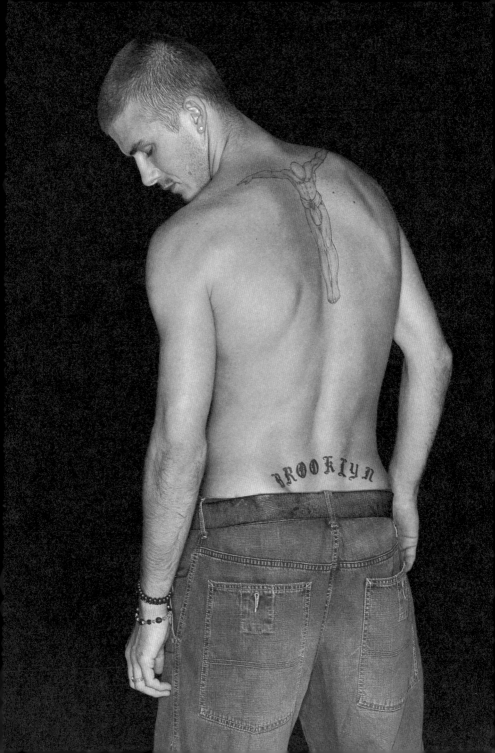

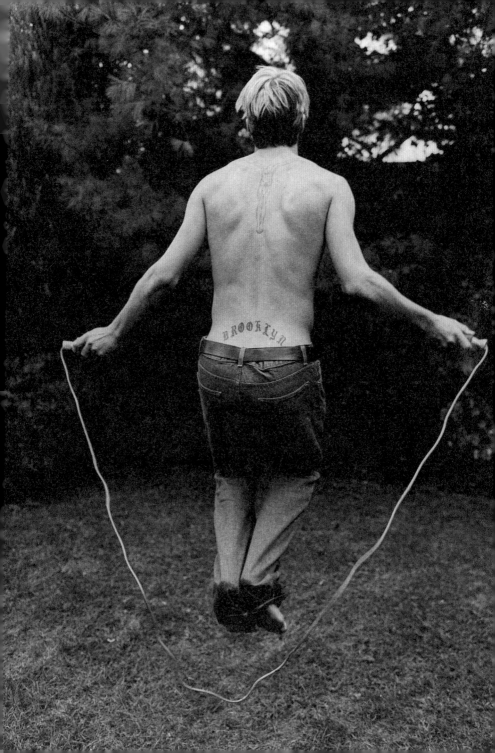

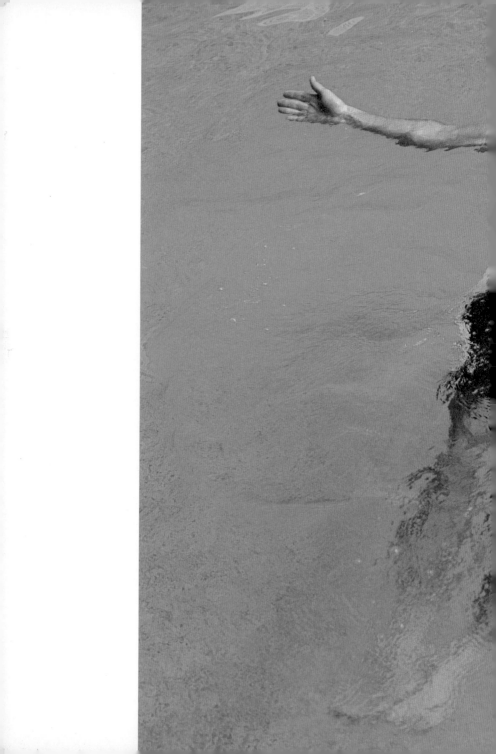

Thank you to my Mum and Dad, Joanne, Lynne and Georgina, my Nan and Grandad, Jackie, Tony, Christian, Louise and Liberty, Matt Dickinson, Rebecca Cripps, Dean Freeman, Alan Edwards, Caroline McAteer and everyone at The Outside Organisation, Tony Stephens, Helen Hollier and everyone at SFX, Sir Alex Ferguson and everyone at Manchester United Football Club, David Gardiner, Andrew Thompson, Nancy Phillips and everyone at Spice HQ, everyone at Adidas UK and all at Hodder & Stoughton

Dean Freeman would like to dedicate his work on this book to the lasting memory of Amanda W. Brown

Dean and Grace would also like to thank David, Victoria and Brooklyn, Jackie and Tony Adams, Nancy Berry, Richard Brown, Collyhurst Boxing Academy, Rebecca Cripps, Mark Cumming, Jean-Michel Dentand, Toby Dodson, Don's Barbers, Helen Harper, Hodder & Stoughton Commissioning Editor Roddy Bloomfield and Production Director Elizabeth Hallett, Alette Jessen-Bruun (Metro Art), Derek Johnson, Mick Jones (colour prints), Diana Law, Catherine Lutman, Manchester United Football Club, Terri Manduca, Steve Macleod (B+W prints), Metro Imaging, Nancy Phillips, Emma Poole, Ken Ramsden, Jo Rickson, Katy Schwartz, Tony Stephens and Andrew Thompson

Text by David Beckham
assisted by Matt Dickinson and Rebecca Cripps

Photography and book concept by Dean Freeman
Art direction by Dean Freeman and Grace

Edited, designed and produced by Grace
Book agent Grainne Perkins at Grace

Published by Hodder & Stoughton